FLYING AND DYING

TOM HUITEMA

Copyright © 2024 by Tom Huitema

All rights reserved.

No portion of this book may be reproduced in any form without written permission from the publisher or author, except as permitted by U.S. copyright law.

Copyright © 2024 by Tom Huitema

Acknowledgements

When you know who your friends are.

Falling from heaven is much easier when caught by loving arms.

My deepest gratitude to those who supported me and were there when we needed them most.

Joy Highhouse offered strength and support as my mind recounted the initial events of my afterlife experience. Her husband Ken Highhouse kept our family informed as the hours passed.

I'm forever indebted to the Portage Fire / Safety Team, Pride Care Ambulance service, and its responders and medics, who saved me.

In the category of best neighbors ever, a shout out to Rita and Dinesh Patel, who comforted everyone with warmth and compassion on the night of my sudden cardiac arrest.

Thanks to one of my oldest and dearest friends, Tom Postula, and his wife Rosella and to the true wealth of friends who called and visited.

Highest regards to the flight department leadership of American Airlines. They helped carry me through my challenges as I sorted the broken pieces of a career I loved. VP of Flight Captain Russ Moore (ret), former Area Director of Flight Captain Tim Raynor, ORD Director of Flight Captain Bill Sponsler, and former Director of Pilot Hiring Captain Cory Glenn acted far beyond the duties of their roles. Perpetuating that capable leadership is VP of Flight Captain Alan Johnson with the assistance of Managing Director of Flight, Captain Bill Sherrod, and Director of Line Ops, Captain Jeff Price.

Combining hard work, diligence and well-placed doses of contagious laughter are my wonderful friends and colleagues with the AA Pilot Hiring Team -Senior Manager of Pilot Hiring, Dena Payne Smith, Captain Nic Brice, Christina Crowl, Eddie Lumpkin, Sarah Chillag, Julie Kabel, Donya Strother, Cassidy Pathammavong , and Donte Rose. They've helped me pave a new path forward while making me feel loved and welcomed. Thank you also to Captain Jim Glick, the Pilot Interview Standards Team, and our great group of pilot interviewers.

My hat is off to the Allied Pilots Association and its dedicated committees. Marsha Reeke RN, whose compassion and support along with the Aeromedical and the Medical Advisors teams have been a pinnacle in my recovery. Thanks to Captain Tim O'Meara, Disabled Pilots Awareness Subcommittee and to all the committee volunteers who assist us during our most challenging times. The strength of commitment and the unity of APA's members attest to it being the world's finest pilot union.

Dedicated to the four pillars of my life.
I love you from here to heaven and all places in between.
Desiree, Savannah, Sophia, and Christian.
With loving regard to my mother, father, brother, and sister.
And eternal love for Hope and Faith.

Contents

Prologue	XI
PART ONE – FLYING	1
1. Career Ender Arrested Development	3
2. When Opportunity Rolls Finding Purpose	10
3. The Box with Wings It's hip to be square.	19
4. Bad Posture The Benefits of Slouching	31
5. The Jurassic Jet Silver hair and silver birds.	36
6. The Left Seat It's Captain Tom	41
7. When Hands Fly Put up your Dukes	52
8. Nosedive Not doing as you're told.	57

9.	The Ambassador Smiles Everybody, Smiles	66
10.	Help Wanted The Peacekeeper	72
11.	Different Feathers Getting Along with Others	76
12.	Help Needed Pilot Assistance Evolves	80
13.	Stepping Up The National Committee	84
14.	Shanghai Surprise Fists of Fury	91
15.	A Hot One From Quiet to Chaos	95
16.	Captain, Be the Captain. Plays Well with Others	101
17.	On Call Drinking the Tea	106
PART TWO – DYING		113
18.	Final Flight Barrel Roll	115
19.	Fit to Die You Only Live Twice	120
20.	Death Grip A Rough Night	124

21. Afterlife 132
    Going Places
22. Your Heart Stopped 137
    ICU to the Recovery Room
23. Spirit Form 142
    Afterlife is kind of like a box of chocolates. You never what you're gonna get.
24. Explaining the Unexplainable 148
    Bonus Territory
25. Reload 157
    Boatbuilding 101
26. In a Heartbeat 163
    Wings and Things
27. The Airway Ahead 166
    A Legacy
28. Four Letter Words 169
    The Art of Interviewing
29. The Influencer 179
    The Responsibility of Recognition
30. Great Circle Route 185
    Ending in the Beginning
31. What Changed and What Didn't 189
    Filling the Dash.
32. Ear Opener 194
    Going With the Flow

33.	The Triple Crown	196
	The Right Side of Bed	
34.	Someday	201
	The Beginning at the End	
Epilogue		203

Prologue

The captain's seat of a Boeing 787 Dreamliner delivers a nice view. A curved windowpane slopes past my left shoulder, inviting me to take in the ever-changing scenery. Pressing my cheek to the glass allows me to look back and barely see the outer edge of the aircraft's composite wingtip. It flexes upward obediently, helping carry the weight of an aircraft structure filled with fuel, cargo, crew, and nearly three hundred souls onboard.

I did it. I got to be an airline captain. With the innocent optimism of a child, I dreamt this would someday be me. That boy still speaks to me under the guise of an aging pilot. "This is sooo cool," he says. I confirm his presence with a smile, letting his tiny voice find my heart and share our love of flying. The child within saw this day but hadn't planned its untimely end.

One night, I lay down in bed and my heart stopped. I died, but I'm feeling much better thanks to CPR and a well-charged set of defibrillator batteries.

During my twenty minutes without a pulse, I borrowed a set of wings only to see them reclaimed. My wings back on Earth had also been clipped. This left me asking that inner child for a hint to the next step. I needed his clear-eyed view of the world.

He sent me back decades, dictating the chapters of my life like tiny time machines. He stitched together the fabric of my past, showing me who I was and who I'd become.

I'm transported to the present day, waking up early to pull fresh thoughts from my mind with the assistance of a strong cup of coffee. I share a group text with two other airline pilots, both also cardiac arrest survivors. We joke about the exclusivity of our club. None of us were aware of our heart conditions, living each day expecting the next. All three of us had time bombs ticking in our chests.

Matt had his cardiac arrest while sitting at the flight controls of a Delta Airlines Boeing 777. His heart stopped after an Atlantic crossing while cruising inbound past the coast of Newfoundland. Captain Te Lee initiated CPR, the aircraft's onboard defibrillating device was used, and a shock later, Matt's heart restarted. He opened his eyes four days later at a hospital in Moncton, Canada to see his wife standing over him.

John bumped into the Grim Reaper one afternoon at a Park City, Utah, ski lodge while suiting up to hit the hills for a snowboarding session. He had the good sense of collapsing in front of an ER nurse with an AED hanging on the wall a few feet away. He, too, was revived and took a helicopter ride from the slopes to a nearby hospital for his recovery.

Out-of-hospital cardiac arrest (OHCA) has an abysmal 10% survival rate and falls even lower if the first shock is delivered after ten minutes. Though CPR can increase those odds, rapid defibrillation is critical within the first several minutes of heart stoppage.

I survived but needed to find my new path.

Writing became my therapy. Emotions became descriptions. Remembrances transformed into words and eased psychological burdens by passing a portion of their weight to the screen in front of me.

In aviation, we often understand an issue more clearly by applying the thirty-six-inch rule. It's a way of saying take a step back, get the big picture, and you may see a solution more clearly. When my words stared back, they allowed the privilege of inspection. They offered laughter, pain, and healing.

I wrote about my cardiac arrest soon after those events to provide the most clarity and accurate detail. My encounter in the presence of God remains chiseled on my heart while the trip there and back slowly yields to the rituals of daily life.

The names of characters, events, and surrounding details have been modified for the purpose of anonymity, artistic license, and privacy. For that reason, I've added the qualifier, it's "Based on a true story." Other than those individuals who have granted me specific permission to use their names and cite their events, any similarity to persons, places, or actual events is purely coincidental. But, in the words of renowned physicist Albert Einstein, *coincidences are God's way of remaining anonymous.*

PART ONE – FLYING

1

CAREER ENDER

ARRESTED DEVELOPMENT

Flashing lights danced atop the police cruiser, illuminating the inside of my car in a parade of red and blue. Below the steering wheel, I held a joint between the tip of my finger and thumb as an open bag of marijuana leaned awkwardly in my lap.

Angst hung in the air, replacing the joviality of moments earlier.

A pulse pushed against my temples and thoughts raced, but one led the charge: career-ender. Did I just flush away years of education?

The squad car lights signaled more than the officer's presence. They signaled the death of my fledgling pilot career.

Hours earlier, I'd trained my last flight school student at the Allegheny County Airport. Long shadows cast from hangars, signaling the close of the day. I yanked the terry cloth tie from around my neck and drove down the ramp to our maintenance facility to see my friend Billy. He worked as a certified A & P airplane mechanic. I made it a habit to check in with him after a transitional girlfriend had dumped him. Her revealing hourglass shape and flirty disposition had spelled trouble from the start, and when she left him for a thicker wallet, he sulked like he'd lost the world.

I found him lounging in the compact cabin of a twin-engine Cessna, engulfed in a cloud of smoke. Billy's knack for self-obliteration had notched up since the breakup.

"Hey Billy, looks like you're done for the day."

"Yeah, I don't feel like fixing anything," he said, peering through slits of eyes. Not that he could anyway, given his present state.

"I'm gonna cruise over to Greater Pitt. Someone told me about a perimeter access road next to the runway. Wanna go check it out?"

"Sure, I'll bring some weed," answered Billy, looking at me with a divergent stare.

We trekked across town to the Greater Pittsburgh International Airport. Consulting hand-scribbled directions, we navigated a few turns and located an unassuming road running along the tight boundary of the airport fence. A track of low-flying aircraft led us to a point just short of a runway threshold. Such hidden gems are high-level paydirt for a plane spotter or aviation enthusiast.

We'd arrived to find a bunch of good-natured hooligans leaning against a Pontiac Firebird and staring at the night sky. They gave us a welcoming nod and returned to their spirited conversation. The covert spot wasn't so secret after all, but the intel on the quality of the view proved accurate, and I was mesmerized.

We stood beneath a blanket of star-salted heavens. Every few minutes, the roar of jet engines tore through the tranquility of the night sky. Landing aircraft strafed overhead by only a couple of hundred feet. The vantage point allowed us to look straight up and see the glow of red anti-collision beacons illuminating the aircraft bellies. These machines transformed kerosene into noise, and while others covered their ears, I embraced the sound as if listening to a rock concert.

Across the street, a rotund hillbilly rounded the Firebird and reached into a cooler in the trunk, pulling out an Iron City Beer.

I yelled, "You guys wanna trade a couple of beers for a joint?"

"Deal!" the guy shouted through a half rack of rotten teeth.

We'd share the spot, enjoy the view, and partake in a little feast among aviation enthusiasts. Perfect.

Still half-baked from earlier, Billy fumbled with the rolling paper, attempting to assemble our end of the arrangement.

"Is it really *that* hard to roll a joint? Give me the weed," I said.

Billy handed me the papers and a crumpled Ziploc baggie containing about four fingers of bunk weed.

I opened the car door and plopped down into the vinyl bucket driver's seat of my 1977 Mercury Bobcat. Mercury's version of the Ford Pinto, the Bobcat, shared its sibling's unsightly appeal and propensity to burst into flames when impacted by a significant rear-end collision—something about the exposed gas tank. Embarrassingly underpowered, it struggled to scale the shallowest Western Pennsylvania hills. But on frigid mornings, the four-cylinder carbureted engine would sputter, cough, and start. It got me to work. And to exotic locales such as this one.

My fingertips plucked buds from the baggie and sprinkled them across the rolling paper. I peered into my lap through the darkness and tightened the ends of the bud with a quick spin, contemplating my unmarketable talent for rolling a joint with my eyes closed.

My deliberations were interrupted as a car rounded the bend with its headlights off. It topped the hill mound and pulled nose-to-nose with my front bumper. That's when it lit up like a Christmas tree, bright high beams and overhead reds and blues. I stared ahead like a deer caught in the police cruiser's headlights.

I froze. My heart sank. Everything I had worked for could vanish in this instant.

No. Sudden. Moves.

The bag of weed remained perched in my lap as the joint trembled in my hand. I leaned forward slightly, allowing my arms to move below the elbows. I didn't want to alarm the police officer, who glared through my front windshield, assessing the situation.

I gently placed the joint into the baggie and felt for the bottom of the seat cushion, mentally measuring enough clearance. I needed to flick the contraband under the driver's seat and away from eyes that would soon probe "plain sight" of the vehicle's interior. My aim betrayed me as the bag missed its mark and turned upside down, spilling across the floorboard. The beam of the officer's flashlight would unquestionably spot it.

The officer stepped out of the cruiser, flashlight in hand.

The words "career ender" again shouted in my mind. The mark of drug possession could not be erased from a pilot's record, and I'd never join the ranks of the aviators passing overhead. At that moment, I hated myself for my arrogance, exhaling as angst clutched my chest.

With the squad car's lights still lighting up my face, I mocked a puzzled surprise as if curious about the purpose of his unanticipated presence. The officer pointed his finger at me and made a flicking motion, directing me to exit the vehicle. I popped open the door and slowly stepped out, trying to mask my uneasiness.

Greater Pittsburgh Airport fell into the same county jurisdiction as Allegheny County Airport, the location of my flight school. The officer's uniform and car displayed an eerie familiarity with those I saw daily at the county airfield. On a routine perimeter patrol, he'd rounded with his headlights off to assess the situation before lighting the place up. Our viewing spot was a secret to no one, especially not the Allegheny County PD.

In 1982, a respectful disposition could sway an officer's decision to assert authority. He considered the totality of the situation and again turned his attention to me. I looked out of place, still wearing the collared shirt and slacks from instructing earlier that day.

The next sixty seconds could change the direction of my life.

"Hello, officer," I offered.

He got right to the point, fatherly but stern.

"What are you up to, son?"

"Plane spotting, sir. I'm a flight instructor at Allegheny County Airport and came to watch airplanes. Officer Don Moore mentioned this was a nice spot." A nervous pitch filled my voice.

I wanted to pull back the namedrop. Damn, that sounded desperate.

His brows settled as he continued to observe me, noting my clean-cut appearance while discerning my choice of words. A look of familiarity evened his gaze, replaced with steely authority.

"Get in your car and get the hell out of here!"

"Yes, sir. Come on, Billy."

We pulled away, and he turned his attention to the baffled beer drinkers standing around the Pontiac.

I've heard it said that God protects children and fools. I've fallen firmly into both categories. But one day, we're made to answer for our choices through statute or karma.

I frequently relived the drive home, recalling the beat of my heart thumping within the numbness that filled my body. Billy didn't break the silence despite the sobering shock, aware of my need for silent trepidation.

I had been in precarious situations previously and stealthily exited a side door as authorities arrived. Arrogance and perceived invincibility are dangerous companions. You can't always stay a step ahead of authority. No one always gets a pass. My luck had run out, but somehow, the officer had granted a reprieve.

That night marked a turning point in my life. If I wanted to be an aviator, I needed to commit to the disciplines of learning my trade and the integrity that came with its immense responsibility. The pilots flying overhead at Greater Pitt made that commitment, and if I ever wished to join them, I had to clean up my act.

Nearly 15 years later, as an airline captain on a Boeing 727, a glimpse of that evening beckoned me, seeking penance. Wanting to close the loop, I interviewed for a position as a reserve police officer for the Portage Police Department in Portage, Michigan.

I graduated as a salutatorian of the Kalamazoo County Reserve Police Academy and spent the next decade of days off volunteering in service of my community. Volunteer work involving a bulletproof vest seemed extreme but provided a new perspective while linking me to an old one. It also allowed me to give back for all I'd been given.

On quieter nights, we'd patrol hidden spots considered a refuge from probing eyes. When we came upon vehicles in those not-so-secret spots, we'd encounter occupants who had embraced a familiar lifestyle defined by youthful arrogance and invincibility. Thankfully, I'd become adept at discerning when dealing with a good person making bad decisions.

With flashlight in hand, I walked up to a young man pale with anxiety. I could see it in his eyes – the regret, the fear, the unasked question: "Did I just ruin my career/life/future?"

I knew what to do then. I pointed the flashlight away from his frightened face and said,

"Let's talk for a minute."

A minute that could change the course of his life.

2

WHEN OPPORTUNITY ROLLS

FINDING PURPOSE

My hands guarded near the flight controls, trying not to intervene.

"More rudder, Rossco!" I shouted.

We rounded out for landing in a howling crosswind as our Cessna 172 began to track away from the centerline. An air-filled windsock saluted perpendicular to the runway heading, attesting to the gust.

"I got this," Ross Wilson said with an intense look of self-assurance.

"It's your wrestling match, buddy. Just don't bonk the runway edge lights."

Crosswind landings offered an additional challenge to disabled pilots. Ross had his hands full with fifteen to twenty knots pushing from the left but wasn't about to let the airplane get away from him. He swung the specialized hand control far right while leaning the left wing into the wind. The device depressed the right rudder as the aircraft regained runway alignment.

"There you go. Good job," I encouraged.

The upwind main wheel touched just left of the centerline as the airplane settled to the pavement.

"Nice," I said as he held the wings' ailerons into the wind, and the airplane decelerated.

I liked to work Ross to the outer edge of his comfort zone. As a natural aviator, he faced every challenge and consistently answered with a commanding touch.

Several months earlier, Metro Air Incorporated had hired me as a flight instructor, and the desire to use my new teaching skills met with frustration. I stared out the flight school's north windows for many empty weeks waiting for my first student to walk through the door.

Despite its favorable location, the school struggled. I had no base salary and was compensated only for the time I flew. I'd only netted a few hundred dollars for giving plane rides during my first eight weeks of employment. When we did fly, the owner sometimes hesitated to pay the instructors. Keeping the lights on outranked my gas money to get to and from the airport.

Even so, I felt rich compared to my previous standard of wealth. At age 14, I'd worked at C&D Television & Appliance for a sub-minimum wage of $1.25 per hour; five hours of cleaning and mopping floors earned me a $6.25 paycheck. The proprietors knew lots of people needed work and cut minimum wage by more than half, knowing that if I didn't take the job, somebody else would.

Flight instructors were also a dime a dozen, so our presence on the property was necessary in case opportunity knocked. When someone signed up at the school, the instructors clamored over who would teach the new student.

"It's my turn; you got the last student!" one instructor would demand.

"That guy quit after the third lesson, so he doesn't count," the other would retort.

Some pilots defined this time as "putting in your dues" until the next bigger, better thing presented itself. I refused to see it this way, nor did I want that to be how I remembered my time as a flight instructor. I'd decided long ago to do all I could to remember as many steps of my aviation path as possible, and this step needed to matter.

My role at Metro Air was often like a sales job.

"Go work the fence!" Betty Peters would say encouragingly. "Elaine just signed up a discovery flight."

"Did you hire me as an instructor or a salesperson?" I'd tease.

She shared a motherly smile while nodding toward the door.

I looked outside to see a half dozen people standing along the terminal fence line. They'd come to the airport to watch airplanes, and as one of the country's busiest corporate airfields, various small jets came and went throughout the day. A conversation could lead to a plane ride or someone signing up for flight lessons. The engagement didn't bother me; I happily spoke to others about airplanes.

I took special note of a gentleman in a wheelchair, often sharing my view just ahead of the flight line. I walked out and greeted him for no reason other than to make his acquaintance.

A Westinghouse corporate Learjet had just departed. Its thunderous exit and unmatched performance drew everyone's attention as it rocketed away.

"You like Learjets?" I opened.

"Yeah," he said, watching the aircraft become a dot in the sky. "I like the 35 series more than the 25. The bigger engines look better."

Ross knew airplanes.

"They're much more efficient, too," I agreed.

Ross was one of the most remarkable people I'd ever met, and we quickly became close friends. He was a non-conformist eager to disagree with the unnatural flow of authority and bureaucracy, backing his words with concise and adept reasoning. Full-shouldered and thick-armed, the power of his presence extended beyond the confines of his wheelchair.

One afternoon, while having lunch, Ross shared the story that led to his paraplegia.

"I've always wanted to be a pilot," he said. "Years ago, I was accepted to Embry-Riddle Aeronautical University."

He paused as the past spoke to him.

"I came home to get my stuff and bring it to the campus in Daytona Beach. They had me scheduled to start classes and flight training the following week."

The shape of his face changed as he stared down, narrowing his eyes.

"The day before I was set to leave, I went for a motorcycle ride. Two cars crashed in front of me, and I couldn't stop. I hit the wreckage and catapulted from the bike. My body hit a tree trunk, and it broke my back. My spine didn't break. Just bruised, but my brain lost the signal to my legs, and I've been a gimp in this wheelchair ever since."

Despite the dark memory, Ross immediately perked up and changed the subject to volley a random insult at something ridiculous. He didn't have it in him to stay sad and had a way of making others laugh no matter what the circumstance. He used a personal creed armed with sometimes twisted logic, reflective of his brilliance, to say nearly anything and get away with it.

"Well, let's see if there's a way to get you in an airplane," I said, returning to the subject.

"Yeah, that would be great," he replied.

We researched and found a certified hand control designed to attach to the rudder pedals of a single-engine Cessna.

We had it shipped from Tennessee and anxiously awaited its arrival, having little to no idea what to expect.

The device showed up a few weeks later in a cardboard box with no instructions and no manual. The thing was a curved bar with a ring on one end, a small, welded crossbar with a couple of clamps, and dangling J-shaped hook on the other.

"What do you think, Ross?" I asked, unsure what to do with it.

"Looks pretty simple," he said as he clamped it over the tops of the left-side rudder pedals. It fit perfectly, the bar angling up like an appendage to the throttle quadrant, topped with a metal ring.

Ross pulled himself into the left seat of the airplane with ease, slid the seat forward, and stowed his wheelchair behind him.

"Let's do this!" he said.

"Okay, but how in the world do we work this thing?"

I jumped into the right seat and looked down at the long bar, still feeling trepidation.

I realized I'd also have to learn to use the hand control, especially if I planned to teach others. Time for some on-the-job training. I pulled my feet away from the right-side rudder pedals. I waved the top of the bar side to side and then up and down, trying to get a feel for it.

"Yeah, Rossco, let's make this happen."

Minutes later, we taxied to the active runway while experimentally turning and stopping the airplane on the ground. The next step would encompass air work, learning, and then teaching a multitude of maneuvers. Together, we'd learn to fly without the use of our legs.

The dream began to unfold.

I've heard of kids who sit at a piano and begin to play and savants who effortlessly learn languages to native levels. Ross's natural gift was flight. He'd picked up from the moment before hitting the tree trunk and reacquainted himself with the passionate aviator waiting inside. Ross demonstrated an unparalleled ability to learn and adapt. The airplane became an extension of him.

On a clear morning, we did some air work and returned for some touch-and-go landings. My hands didn't once need to touch the controls. We taxied back to the ramp and stopped the airplane; I knew Ross was ready for his first solo flight.

"Go take a lap around the pattern. I'll see you back here in a few minutes."

He shot me a look of confidence; he had worked hard for this day.

With half its former payload gone, the plane leaped into the air after a short ground roll. Fifteen minutes later, Ross pulled into the ramp and shut down the engine. I opened the door to see tears flowing from his eyes.

"How did it feel?" I said, asking the obvious.

"It flies a lot better without your big ass in it," he croaked out through intense emotion.

Between his personality and ubiquitous presence, he became the talk of the airport and the town. He loved to fly. He *lived* to fly.

A neighboring flight school, Steel City Aviation, headed by Mark Schreiner, joined to empower the program. Struggling business owners set aside rivalries, selflessly opening their hearts with an outpouring of love over profit.

For those of limited financial ability, Schreiner allowed the airplane to fly for the price of gas. Business owners like Mark saw the opportunity to support humanity and did so selflessly.

Ross soon earned a Private Pilot License and continued to a Commercial Pilot License with Instrument Rating, effortlessly acing all his FAA check rides.

The disabled program grew, spawning the roots of the Pennsylvania Wheelchair Pilots Association. It quickly drew media attention, and The Pittsburgh Press picked up the story; it proliferated when others read or heard about the program. People with paraplegia, amputees, and other disabled pilots joined the ranks. I taught more pilots with disabilities than fully ambulatory students.

Ross insisted upon independence for all who took part in the program. One day, he eyed a disabled student who brought someone to aid him in and out of the airplane.

"This is about independence," Ross offered as a gentle reminder.

I penciled a flying lesson onto the calendar as he disregarded Ross and looked at his assistant.

"Can you make it that day?" he asked his helper.

"I don't think you understood me. Leave your slave at home!" Ross fired. His formidable presence radiated.

The guy got the message and returned for a flight lesson by himself a week later.

I'd learned a simple lesson. Few of life's true successes are attached to monetary gain. If anything, money is an uncalibrated meter. Looking back 40 years later, I can note that everyone's willingness to give time and attention to this program at their own selfless expense significantly contributed to its success.

During this era, and sadly even continuing unto this day, society often dismissed people with disabilities and pushed them into a corner.

"The rehab people told me I could repair watches," Ross once recounted. "I wasn't going to be pushed aside. It made me more rebellious, knowing I had to find something that unshackled me, especially after losing the use of my legs."

The wheelchair pilots program replaced artificial boundaries with empowerment. It was a form of freedom once only reserved and experienced by fully ambulatory people. Those with disabilities, could now also fulfill the dream of flight. The tear-filled eyes of disabled pilots after their first solo flights were not just a tribute to having partaken in the wonder of flight but to their freedom.

I'm reminded of the adage, "When the student is ready, the teacher will appear." I may have taught Ross how to fly, but my interactions with him taught me about life. They provoked my uncommon perspectives and refocused my intention. The redirection in my life resulting from my coming to God moment back along the fence line at Greater Pitt Airport had opened the curtain to the next stage of my flying career.

As it turned out, it wasn't who walked through the door that changed my life, but who rolled by it. To this day, it's been some of the most fulfilling flying of my career.

Ross Wilson passed quietly among friends in the summer of 2022. His resilient spirit, love of aviation, and legacy remain forever in our hearts.

Ross Wilson, Tom Huitema and Steve Schindler

3

THE BOX WITH WINGS

IT'S HIP TO BE SQUARE.

"Your ass is going to be in the chief pilot's office explaining what a screwball you are!" screamed Bill McCloud. It was my second trip at Pennsylvania Commuter Airlines / Allegheny Commuter. The Williamsport, Pennsylvania crew base had a couple of hotheads, and McLoud topped the list as a red-faced temper tantrum-prone bullhorn. I'd neglected to pull the chock from ahead of the left main wheel, thinking it was a ground crew function. We throttled up and jumped the chock - problem solved. Bill's hysterical outburst from such an inconsequential event planted a seed at a deeper level.

"I'm never going to be like that," I mumbled below the rumble of the propellors, guilty only of visualizing mopping the ramp with this guy.

After a fulfilling stint as a flight instructor back at Allegheny County Airport, it was time to move on. Penn Airlines, a Harrisburg-based USAir feeder, hired me as a first officer/copilot. I'd learn from good pilots and bad actors, taking inventory of who and what I'd eventually be as a pilot.

The Shorts 330 was the first multi-engine turbine-powered commercial transport I would fly. My buddies liked to poke me about its lack of curb appeal.

"That thing is so ugly it flies by repelling the ground.", one friend said.

"I know," I'd respond. "She's a bit homely, but she's my baby, and I love her."

Produced in Belfast, Ireland, the Shorts 330 and its single-tail sibling, the 360, came fully equipped with a catalog of insulting nicknames: the Belfast Bomber, the Flying Shed, and the Skypig, to name a few. Based on its predecessor, the Skyvan, some joked that this flying machine might have been designed in an Irish pub.

The airplane sustained flight by the most unconventional combination of aerodynamic principles. Long and straight wings attached to the top of a cambered fuselage and combined with a flat bottom. The body functioned as a primitive airfoil and generated a small portion of the aircraft's lift. Semi-retractable landing gear mounted beneath the outer edges of stub wings technically made it a bi-wing airplane.

The harmony of these oddities added to this contraption's ability to achieve flight with a payload. Despite its complete lack of curb appeal, the Shorts fulfilled its purpose well. It held thirty or more passengers and a flight attendant, tightly squeezed into a cabin that resembled a shipping container. The fuel tanks sat over the passenger cabin, a notable detail that wasn't mentioned on the emergency briefing card. The interior ironically involved a collaboration with Boeing.

Flying scheduled routes around Pennsylvania became my home turf for the next couple of years.

I'd graduated to Greater Pitt Int'l Airport, now on the right side of the fence while also keeping my promise to stay on the right side of the law. I shared the Greater Pitt stage with USAir pilots, albeit at a commuter carrier. My airplane didn't exude a sleek aerodynamic design, but flying a pretty plane didn't rank anywhere on my list of prerequisites.

I wore my first pilot uniform and gleamed when I walked through the terminal. My jacket had three stripes on the sleeve and a shiny set of wings with the letters PCA (Pennsylvania Commuter Airlines) pinned to the left pocket. Real pilot stuff.

As I stood outside beneath a jet bridge, a catering truck rolled up and sounded a quick honk.

"Hey, Joey," I said.

"Found some untouched meals on a galley cart. You want 'em?"

"Heck yeah. I'll put the extras in the ops area."

He passed down a stack of aluminum foil-covered plastic plates, and I handed him a USA Today newspaper I'd scavenged from a gate. Passengers often left them behind when boarding their flights.

"Premium grade," I said. "Only been read once, and the crossword hasn't been touched."

My commuter flying gig didn't pay much, allowing the lowest barter level. With a full belly, I waddled to the ramp for a cup of airplane coffee, followed by a preflight inspection of the airplane.

The Shorts looked solid as I completed the walk-around. I learned not to get too close to the downwind side of either engine. Oil would often blow off the cowling and grease a clean pilot shirt. Aircraft of this era were known to have a degree of inherent leakage. This one excelled in regurgitating fluids and spit on me like an angry camel whenever the opportunity presented itself.

As I completed my oil dodging preflight, Captain James Conrad Kause pulled open his cockpit window and called toward me.

"Hey, UM, go get the passengers."

"I'm on it."

Once again, my flying duties extended beyond the operation of the aircraft.

My baby face had won me the nickname "UM," an acronym for "Unaccompanied Minor," the designation given to young passengers traveling alone.

I'd barely reached the legal drinking age, yet I flew passengers on a scheduled commercial revenue route. It didn't help that I looked much younger than my twenty-one years.

I took a courtesy van back over to the terminal. After calculating the flight's weight and balance data, I needed to coax a gate agent to board my flight. The passengers stepped onto a small bus, and we transported them to a ramp area to board the airplane. The short ride could prove entertaining. Granted, the age comments made by passengers were endless, but I wore them like badges.

"You're the pilot? Did the school bus drop you off?" someone would jab.

"No sir, my mom brought me. She's the captain," I'd answer.

Jaws dropped as the shuttle bus approached the Shorts, squatting awkwardly on the ramp.

"That's our airplane? It looks like the box another airplane came in. Can that thing land on water?"

"Yes, but only once," I'd reply.

"How does it even fly?"

"You remember how Dorothy's house flew in The Wizard of Oz? It's kinda like that."

I never minded the interactions, especially once I'd fine-tuned my comebacks.

All boarded and buttoned up, I plopped into the right seat of a roomy, oddly accommodating flight deck for our daily hop from Pittsburgh to State College, Pennsylvania.

I no longer heard the pop and sputter of piston engines as the whistle of the Pratt and Whitney PT-6 motors signaled my graduation to a turbine-powered aircraft. The sound of its low idle, fully feathered propeller blades paddling effortlessly against the air reminded me of other aircraft of the time. This airplane had a restless shake even when not in motion. Moving the propellers to a lower pitch allowed RPM to increase and send its bite of air aft, conveying the intention of forward movement. Though some love the smell of jet fuel in the morning, the sound of engines has always made my heart skip a beat. Their strength first allowed humankind to fly and soon propelled aircraft at unimaginable speeds.

The jet blast of larger aircraft pushed against our fuselage as we taxied to the departure runway.

Earlier that day, a hawk had startled me by swooping by the aircraft's right side on our approach to landing. It now perched on a taxiway sign next to the runway threshold as if granting each aircraft permission to depart.

"Hey Jim, check out the hawk. That's the dude that strafed us on short final when we came in."

"Yeah, that's Rex. He lives here." Jim replied nonchalantly.

"Even birds mess with this airplane."

"It's Rex's airport, and he puts up with us."

The daily flight between Pittsburgh and State College proved monotonous by route but challenging by weather.

The Shorts' boxed shape forbade a pressurized cabin, necessitating low-altitude flight. It didn't hold ice well and, with its flat sides, equated to a wrestling match in a crosswind. With no autopilot, we hand flew from the moment the throttles advanced to takeoff power until decelerating on our destination runway. Flying the airplane was a full-time job, and even enjoying a cup of coffee could be a balancing act.

The twin tail with yaw damper barely countered the airplane's constant desire to squirm, necessitating crew members and passengers display intestinal fortitude. Even during non-turbulent level flight, any movement in the back of the airplane, from the flight attendant rolling her galley cart forward for beverage service to a passenger using the aft lavatory, necessitated a commensurate pitch input via the control column combined with pitch trim setting. Because their stroll to the back of the cabin moved the center of gravity aft, I sometimes held the forward column input, hoping the person would be quick to use the lav. Constantly retrimming the airplane felt tedious. Theoretically, when they returned to their seat, the pitch trim would be correct again, but this was not often the case.

When we had a particularly active passenger cabin, the flight required constant control input to counter the passengers' movement. Evening flights were typically better as weary passengers would be more likely to remain seated, but this was still a plane you never stopped flying.

I may have been a competent professional during this season of my pilot life, but I retained a sense of my juvenile self. Like a kid given the keys to a Corvette who can't resist the temptation to stomp the gas pedal, my comfort with the airplane summoned a desire to push it around a little.

Despite the aircraft's bulky size, its counterweighted ailerons equated to an impressive roll rate. One evening, I complied with ATC's turn instructions and snapped the airplane into a quick bank, envying the roll response.

"Hey, Tom," said Captain Dennis Erdman.

"Yeah?"

"You may have just scared that woman in the back of the airplane. She bought your dinner tonight. You owe her the comfort of a smooth turn."

It may have been inconsequential then, but Dennis's words still reside with me. I've shared them with others who display a similar disregard. Many one-off sentences in my life have led to lifelong changes. A graceful manipulation of the flight controls became a habit from that day forward.

The minimum age to attain an Airline Transport Pilot license was 23. I planned to sit back comfortably and enjoy my duties from the right seat while continuing to learn from very knowledgeable and capable captains. By 23, I'd hoped to have enough seniority and experience to transition to the left seat as the pilot in command. Though the transition to captain appeared to be a feasible plan, it did not happen as I'd hoped.

Unlike other commuter carriers, Pennsylvania Airlines pilots liked where they were and had no desire for a career change. The airline had no overnight layovers, so pilots were usually home in time to see their kids walk through the door after school. Having been based in State College, PA, we had either of two trips. One was an early departure to Pittsburgh, PA, with an afternoon return flight. The other was a connection through Harrisburg to Philadelphia and then back. Either version of this trip provided crew members with the ability to be home every night; it had the feel of a regular nine-to-five job. They all saw the benefit of sleeping in their own beds every night, and their salaries were higher than most other commuter regional pilots, adding to their reluctance to move on to a major airline carrier.

I once asked Captain Fred Maurer if he'd applied to the mainline carrier. His answer? "My wife just planted a garden." At the time, it felt like he was speaking Mandarin.

Fred had a light, yet impactful way of putting things. His smile had a gentle way of telling me I had much to learn.

"Wait, what? Do you mean you wouldn't want to make way more money flying bigger jets all over the country while laying over in cool cities?"

"Nope," he replied.

Fred had already explored the world, and as a Vietnam Veteran, had seen more than a few things.

"Being based in Pittsburgh means I'd have to commute."

He already lived where he wanted to be, earned what he needed, and embraced the happiness it brought his wife.

Today, those seemingly random words he spoke – "My wife planted a garden" – make perfect sense.

Many of the pilots at Pennsylvania Airlines shared a similar perspective, feeling content where they were.

The minimal attrition led to sluggish upward movement, and while other commuter carriers were upgrading captains within a short time, our advancement stagnated.

I respected this, but after two years and nearly 2000 hours in the right seat, I wanted and needed to take command of an aircraft. I enjoyed flying for Penn Airlines, but a lateral move to a regional airline would become the only way forward.

One afternoon, my old buddy Ray Renshaw called to check-in. The last time I'd seen Ray, we'd been shooting bottle rockets at each other in the hall of an apartment complex. He's that guy whose friendship picks up from the day it left off, no matter how long it's been since the last interaction.

We started every conversation with an obligatory exchange of insults in a thick Pittsburgh accent.

"You mamby milk toast big bucket of…"

"Shut up, you beebly eyed Rodan, looking genetically deficient excuse for a human. What are you doin' up-there in Michigan?"

"Flying! Whadya still doin' down there in PA?"

"Same. My airline's got a lot of lifers, so I can't slide to the left seat."

We'd flight instructed together at the Allegheny County Airport, and he'd found his way to a rapidly expanding regional airline in the Midwest. He told me about his new workplace.

"If you wanna upgrade quick to captain, you oughta come out here. Things are movin' fast," Ray said.

The appeal of fresh geography beckoned. Simmons Airlines offered quick advancement to those with experience, and their fleet included the Shorts 360 aircraft. I applied, and my offering of fleet-specific experience got me the job.

The airline had a different vibe. The young pilots, flight attendants, and variety of layovers resembled an airborne frat house. Crewmembers found their way to each other's rooms on the overnights and usually not to sleep. I'd transitioned from a stoic married bunch to a rowdy single crowd who never missed an opportunity to have a good time. The lateral step to Simmons paid off within two months. I received the award of captain on the Shorts, a step I couldn't accomplish in over two years back at Pennsylvania Airlines. The flying took me to high-density traffic areas like Detroit Metro and Chicago O'Hare while continuing to challenge and build my skills in Northern Michigan and its Upper Peninsula.

The Shorts SD3 type certificate was the first of ten type certifications I would earn throughout my career. Now twenty-three, I held the reins and commanded my first scheduled passenger aircraft. I'd been entrusted with the safe transport of a crew and thirty-six passengers and embraced the responsibility, even if I wasn't old enough to rent a car at the destination airport.

I'd become adept with the airplane I'd called home for the past couple of years, now incorporating those skills in a different environment. My first authentic taste of the left seat provided a dose of a career and character I'd mold around those responsibilities.

I became comfortable with my captain's duties, knowing they represented only a small scale of the challenges I'd eventually tackle on a larger field of play.

★★★

An early winter storm had crossed northern Michigan, lowering landing visibilities while burying the region with snow. Though challenging, the complicated approaches to some smaller airports had become routine. On this day, we arced the Shorts within the obscuration of a thick cloud cover toward our final approach to Alpena airport, hoping to exit the base and land. We broke free from the ragged bottom, skimming beneath the overcast at our minimum descent altitude to see a short snow-blanketed runway in front of us. The edges of the runway barely distinguished themselves with a thin line of lighting.

Accurate runway performance numbers didn't exist due to the lack of braking action reports or other data. We just had to eyeball it.

We lowered the landing gear and flaps, descending toward the runway's approach end with the intention of a sturdy touchdown followed by full propeller reverse and the hope of sufficient braking action. The hair began to stand up on the back of my neck as we neared the threshold.

"I'm not doing this," I said to the first officer. I pushed the throttles forward and commanded a go-around. I wasn't about to slide off the end of this or any other runway.

Topping 3000 hours of flight time, I'd spent three years hand-flying this beast through ice and rain, never more than 10,000 feet above the ground. I'd gotten tossed about like a rag doll in turbulence we couldn't climb away from and wrestled this flat-sided flying machine to the runway in blazing crosswinds. I sweated through my shirts in the summer and shivered on frigid winter mornings, hoping the coffee maker could give me a warm enough splash of joe to warm my hands after they touched the frigid controls.

The Shorts had served its purpose well. It taught me how to fly in adverse environments, manage a flight crew, and work with passengers, agents, and others.

Each line of my flight logbook told a different story, prodded a memory, or spoke of an adventure. Some entries spoke louder than others, but each takeoff equaled a safe landing. On this day, I'd log my last flight on the Shorts, having paved the path to the next chapter.

A short time later, we landed on the nicely cleared runway of our alternate of Traverse City, Michigan. We pulled onto the ramp area and shut down the engines. I expelled an audible sigh.

First Officer Danny Siciliano looked at me with assuredness. "I'm glad you punched out back there, Tom. That runway gave me the hee-bee gee-bees."

"I'm with you," I said, cracking a smile. "This is actually my last trip. Next week, I'm heading to Ft. Worth, Texas. I got hired at American Airlines."

4

BAD POSTURE

THE BENEFITS OF SLOUCHING

Let's rewind about six months.

I'd misrepresented a number on my pilot application, and the moment of truth was upon me. The discovery of one simple fact would negate my consideration for employment. It was crunch time in the most literal sense.

I'd flown to Dallas / Ft. Worth for the first of a three-phase multi-day screening process at American Airlines. Most applicants didn't make it past this stage. USAir still hadn't called, so I understated a number on my app, hoping AA wouldn't catch it.

"Stand against the wall, please," the nurse said with a robotic tone.

I stepped beneath the metal measuring bar. The nurse looked up and lowered the bar to the crown of my head as I condensed my spine with a slouch and pushed my hips out slightly. I stepped away from the device and straightened to my normal height. She wrote: "76" (inches, aka 6'4") on the personnel sheet and flipped it over. I exhaled a sigh of relief.

At 6'5", I exceeded the maximum height for pilot applicants at American Airlines by one inch. Only one other tall pilot before me had accomplished the same feat. Captain John Higley, also 6'5", successfully argued his FAA Medical showed 6'4", prompting the nurse to change the number on his personnel sheet. As of this writing, John is legendary and tops the nearly 16,000 pilot roster at seniority number two. Eating my veggies as a kid almost cost me this job. Though I joke about it now, that one inch could have altered the direction of my life, and it has yet to impede my job functions.

Fellow pilots back at the regional airline referred to AA's screening process as "interview practice" due to the reputed turndown rate. The airline became picky when an influx of unemployed pilots from bankrupt post-deregulation carriers spilled onto the job market. The triviality of an extra inch of height, a slight correctable vision impairment, or a couple of extra pounds around the waistline prompted a rejection. Either that or they wore a necktie of the wrong color.

I'd expected a "thanks but no thanks" letter due to my lack of a four-year degree, so the invitation to a Phase 2 interview came as a surprise.

I returned to Fort Worth, Texas, for AA's renowned astronaut-physical exam. It comprised everything short of removing and inspecting vital organs and took two days to complete.

After checking me for a hernia, the doctor instructed me to step toward a line. With my pants still around my ankles, I hopped toward him.

"Get away from me with that thing!" he shouted.

I had tears in my eyes laughing. Knowing the guy had a great sense of humor broke the tension of an intensive physical exam.

After an EKG, I entered a small room where they conducted a hearing test. With a clicker in my hand, I pushed the button each time I heard a beep or thought I heard a beep. After a series of tones, I no longer heard anything, assuming the test exceeded my audible range. With an endless ringing in my ears, likely obscuring the higher decibel sounds, I contemplated my earlier life exposure to loud music and louder airplanes. Several minutes later, a nurse opened the door to the booth.

"Hi, sorry. We got busy and forgot you were in here."

"That's okay," I replied. "I stopped hearing sounds and thought maybe I just had awful hearing."

She smiled and led me to the EEG room, where they attached little probes to my head. Shortly after, I sat in an administrative interview wearing a blue suit with hair pointed in every direction from the goop of recently attached electrodes.

"Sorry about the glue in my hair," I said.

"No worries," he replied, grinning. "That's pretty much everybody who's not bald."

The "astronaut physical" had gone well, prompting a callback.

A month later, I returned for Phase 3, which entailed flying from the captain's seat of a four-engine Boeing 707 simulator. The largest aircraft I'd flown to date could nearly fit in the cargo compartment of this one. I opted for a "flown one, flown 'em all" theory, piloting this like any other airplane. After a series of maneuvers, including a holding pattern, I hand-flew a precision profile to minimums, requiring a missed approach. During the go-around, an outboard engine failed. The momentum of the failure required a potent punch of the rudder, and my long legs accommodated the task.

A final interview in a small interrogation room with three senior captains followed. These were good old boys, but they knew whom they wanted to let into the club. One badgered me while the other two looked on to see if I'd take the bait.

"So, all you've flown is that boxcar and not even for a year as a captain?"

"I've enjoyed the left seat so far. I've flown in some challenging environments and look forward to continued learning," I said respectfully.

"You hardly look old enough to drive."

Still a baby-faced 23, I barely needed to shave. With a mandatory retirement of 60 back then, I did a quick mental calculation.

"Yes, sir. I've got over 36 years to dedicate to this airline, and I can't wait to get started!"

Captain Grumpy's eyes flickered upward as if doing the calculation himself. He then succumbed to a kick under the table from a fellow interviewer who couldn't help but concede to my unwavering positivity.

I returned home eager for a favorable result but braced for rejection.

My dreams still resided with USAir, who had more amenable hiring criteria. I'd sent them an updated application every three to four weeks for the past two years, even flying to their corporate office in Washington, DC, to get extra application forms. I theorized that my file might stick out because it must have been one of the thickest in the personnel drawer. Even with letters of recommendation, USAir never called. My hometown airline had no interest in me, but the largest airline on earth did.

I called American Airlines a week later to see how I'd done.

"Umm, let me see," said a secretary.

I could hear her fumbling through some paperwork.

"Yes, you're hired."

"Oh my gosh! Thank you." I beamed.

Something in this moment felt understated. The weight of years of hard work carried into the lightness of a voice on the other end of the telephone line. I'd gotten my dream job and had found my home for the next four decades.

5

The Jurassic Jet

Silver hair and silver birds.

Other than the toilets, the only seat that sat sideways on a Boeing 727 was that of the flight engineer. Many early-generation commercial aircraft had three pilots. The captain and first officer shared flying duties, and the third pilot served a non-flying role. They controlled pressurization, paralleled the generators, operated fuel pumps, and completed other tasks associated with aircraft systems. First flown in 1963, the 727 Tri-Jet lacked the automation common to modern aircraft, thus requiring a flight engineer or what other pilots jokingly called a "plumber."

New hire pilots started in the sideways seat until they had enough seniority to transition to the right seat of one of the fleets. The initial training took the pilot from no knowledge to a fully certified flight engineer. The grind of an intensive American Airlines curriculum yielded a high attrition rate. In our class of six, one dropped out early, and another barely made the cut after required retesting. Rumors floated around the Flight Academy of a new hire group losing five of six candidates. I refused to be a part of the fallout and seized days off between classes to keep up with the subject matter, noticing the anguish of new hires who needed that time to tend to domestic responsibilities.

Once I completed training, the reward of a "Flight Engineer Turbojet" certificate added its ink to my FAA licensing. It allowed me to ease into my new assignment by observing the other pilots without taking the flight controls and keeping my head low through my first probationary year.

The 727 was like a Harley-Davidson with wings. Slow climbing and thunderously loud, it set off every car alarm in the airport parking lot when it took off. After years of low altitude flying, the novelty of no longer grinding through weather at low altitudes opened a new dimension. Rather than a short hop from a big city to a small town, the destinations spanned cultures and climates. Some referred to it as 600 mph between parties.

In another eighteen months, I'd upgrade to the co-pilot position. For now, the birds-eye view of my future flying duties educated me about what lay ahead. Getting a feel for the diverse mix of personalities who occupied these flight decks also offered a unique perspective.

In the late 1980s, captains were hard-driving leftovers from the brat pack. They smoked, drank, and aged in dog years. At the time, the mandatory age 60 retirement served a practical purpose as many pilots paid a physical and cognitive toll for their hard-charging lifestyles. By their retirement age, many had little left in the tank.

The list of characters working at the airline during that time reflected a forgotten era. Many captains exuded a Dean Martin swagger or a John Wayne hubris. The instrument panel could catch fire, and they'd dip the tip of their cigar into the flames.

They'd look at you a couple of puffs later and say, "It's getting hot up here. Do we have a checklist for that?"

Others were stone-cold whacky.

One captain claimed he'd encountered a flying disc during his military tenure and had become adamant regarding the existence of aliens. When flying by a thunderstorm, he'd make odd comments.

"They're charging up in there," he'd say, suggesting alien spaceships were tapping power from within the storm.

A moment later, he'd defiantly share another gem.

"I'm going. If they'll take me, I'm out of here," he said, verbalizing his desire to join whatever alien race resided within the storm clouds.

"Screaming Joe Leeming" had a knack for yelling at everyone who crossed his path for the most insubstantial reasons. His thick-lensed glasses magnified the size of his eyes, adding to a bugged-eyed look. He wasn't a bad guy but never learned effective problem-solving and communication, resorting only to elevation.

Once, while eating his crew meal, he chirped up -

"This food is terrible!"

Soon after, Joe turned a light shade of green and headed back to use the forward lavatory, leaving me alone with the first officer, Les Anderson. Les, a guy as cool as a cucumber, spent his days off as a musician. He turned his head toward me.

"Hey Tom, I wonder if Joe got a toilet steak."

"A what?"

"Some flight attendants don't take guff from pilots," he continued. "If you piss them off badly enough, they'll drag a piece of meat around the bowl of the forward lav and throw it back onto the plate."

"Oh, gross!"

"Some words of wisdom, buddy. Never mess with the person who prepares your food."

"Noted, Les. Thanks."

It wouldn't have been beyond Joe to yell at the purser about something inconsequential, contributing to the quality of his dining experience.

Though a colorful bunch, this generation of aviators had begun to retire during my initial years of employment. While they populated our flight decks, I focused on picking up every piece of knowledge they had to share. Even the more eccentric pilots could impart valuable learning despite their off-key opinions. Flying several different aircraft fleets allowed for greater exposure to these aviators across various route structures.

I happily returned to the DFW Schoolhouse to learn any airplane my seniority would allow. In my first seven years of employment, I visited five times to complete qualification requirements on four aircraft, eagerly absorbing anything and everything related to aviation.

With several crew bases to choose from, I transferred using a "two suitcases and a car" rule. If it didn't fit, I'd donate or dispose of it. Disposal could be fun. My buddies and I once threw all my cheap furniture off the third-floor balcony of my apartment. Some of it, especially the particle board pieces, exploded on impact. Mattresses bounced, and box springs tumbled. I remember a couch hitting the ground and holding together like a tank.

An electrician working on the building next door had been watching the debauchery and noticed the strength of the couch. "Can I have that thing?" he asked. We loaded it in the back of his van ten minutes later.

I did some dating but promised myself to maintain freedom of movement without responsibility to another. I wanted my 20s to myself. Despite being forthright, it could cause conflict with those who thought they could change or control me.

"It's really selfish of you not to want to share your life with another," scolded a young lady.

"You're right," I agreed. "I chose to be selfish. I owe this time to myself and no one else."

I boated on freshwater lakes of the Carolinas while flying domestically. After a tornado in Raleigh, NC, destroyed my apartment building, I packed up my battered car and moved to Miami to fly the Central and deep South America routes. Adventures awaited at every corner, and I made it my task to step through as many of the world's gateways as possible. The lifestyle seemed surreal at times.

With an assortment of new aircraft adding to the fleet and pilot retirements vacating positions ahead of me, I received my initial captain upgrade at age 30.

My dream of commanding a large commercial aircraft was within reach.

6

THE LEFT SEAT

IT'S CAPTAIN TOM

I jerked awake from a restless night of sleep early on the morning of my initial captain's checkride. Butterflies swarmed in my stomach. I knew that no matter how much I'd prepared for what lay ahead, this day would offer challenges and yield one of two outcomes. I'd either have a newly inked Fokker F-100 type certificate on my Airline Transport Pilot license or be handed a dreaded pink slip.

A poster depicting the overhead panel of a flight deck hung above my hotel room desk. I looked at it and began reciting systems knowledge attached to each switch. Nervously considering some additional last-minute review, I opened a Flight Ops manual the size of a door stopper.

"By now, either I know this or I don't," I said as I closed the book. The previous five weeks of work had provided ample opportunity to know the new airplane well.

I got dressed and climbed aboard the semi-hourly van to the AA Flight Academy. As I entered, the unspoken embrace of a warm familiarity comforted me. I'd been here numerous times to certify as a first officer on other airplanes. The "Schoolhouse" had challenged and rewarded me for my efforts, but today had a different feel.

First things first – the men's room ceremony. Before any flight check, I'd find my designated oversized stall in one of the simulator building's men's rooms and briefly sanction it as a private house of worship.

"Thank you, God, for my flying abilities. Please help me shine today, yadda, yadda, yadda... Oh, and please also bless these pants because I may have just lowered my knee into something nasty."

With prayers, affirmations, and a combined bathroom break complete – I headed down the long corridor containing arenas of simulator bays. The simulators are designed to teach, hone, and test pilots' skills in a virtual environment. Each sim is also called a box due to its blockish exterior, propped up on six long hydraulic or electric legs, giving it the look of an alien insect.

I walked by the boxes as each leaned in an odd posture to the hiss of pistons. They thrust in every direction via six-axis motion, mimicking whatever phase of flight its occupants experienced at that moment.

I would be testing on the Fokker F100. It was underpowered and slow compared to other airliners. On the other hand, it had a predictable and intelligent design with a clean and impeccably organized flight deck.

Manufactured in my birth country of Holland, it held 100 passengers with a crew of two pilots and two flight attendants. It was thus dubbed the "Dutch Double Date." Due to its underwhelming air conditioning system, they also called it the "Dutch Oven."

As I walked toward the briefing room, an old buddy approached from the other direction. We stopped for a quick chat. Kevin, a California native who surfed anytime he could paddle out, looked contemplative, speaking in his signature long-toned West Coast drawl.

"Hey Tom, did you hear about Rick's ride yesterday?"

"No, everything go okay?"

"Dude, no. The friggin' check pilot downed him."

"Oh, no. Any idea what happened?"

"Total bullshit ride. On his first takeoff, the check pilot launched him into an unrecoverable wind shear, and he crashed off the end of the runway. He's all like, oh my bad, that must have been programmed in there from a previous simulator session. Of course, now Ricky's fried, and how's he gonna pull it together for the next two hours after that?"

"Agh, otherwise, how was the play, Mrs. Lincoln?"

"Exactly. Of course, then the check pilot cranks up his usual ridiculous check ride like nothing happened. They should have called it right then and let Ricky pull himself together. He kept going. The ride went downhill. He ended up gettin' a pink slip. Word is he's not too happy about it."

"You know I've got my ride with the same guy today."

"Well, good luck, man. Don't let him frazzle you."

I felt bad for Rick. He'd been my training partner throughout the schooling, but we had to separate to do our flight checks since we were both captains. He'd easily gotten through everything, and this outcome surprised me.

I'd been eager to learn this new airplane and become a captain, but early in our training, instructors told us we'd face an obstacle.

We'd both been scheduled with a poorly regarded examiner. No more than the luck of the draw, we'd have to deal with a short straw.

The check pilot had a notorious reputation for inventing nearly insurmountable exam scenarios, and his bust rate was epic. When the procedures were successfully completed, he'd stir the pot even more by contriving additional havoc to further push the boundaries on subsequent checkrides. Back in the day, check pilots had the liberty to embellish to the extent they found necessary, and this guy took it to the next level.

The warning sat in the back of my mind, but with the vigorous curriculum and my resolve to do well, I trusted all would work itself out. Both the ground school and simulator phases of training had gone well. I was going to enjoy flying this airplane.

A neatly dressed gentleman entered the briefing room, and after some small talk, we dove into the aircraft systems validation. It all progressed straightforwardly as we elaborated on the nuances of each aircraft system. Two hours later, I'd checked the square on the oral exam portion. Not bad so far, I thought. Dr. Jekyll was about to become Mr. Hyde.

I walked down the gangplank into the simulator and crawled into the left seat.

My first officer, Gabe, served as a "seat filler," already nested in the seat next to me.

As a simulator instructor pilot, his job as the co-pilot (in this setting) was to act as a proficient and capable assistant but not in any way to lead or question my decisions. He would follow any direction I give him, whether correct or incorrect.

"You going to keep me out of trouble today?" I asked.

"I'm here if you need me," Gabe said with a dry indifference.

I held sole responsibility for the outcome of any emergency. Flight deck resource management plays a critical role. The mismanagement of resources can quickly overwhelm the pilots, and overloading the pilot sitting next to you can be just as detrimental as not providing sufficient direction.

The checkride would take place from a virtual Chicago O'Hare Airport. I looked up at the window screens projected in front of me. A Chicago jet bridge and gate number peeked through the 3D display. The familiarity comforted me. Having been domiciled at O'Hare for several years, I considered my previous knowledge of its taxiways, runway configurations, and approach procedures in my favor.

We taxied out and made an uneventful takeoff.

"How bout that?" I said under my breath. No wind shear and no engine failure. I knew some malfunction would soon bring me back to Chicago, and I'd mentally prepared for it. The airplane's annunciator panel lit up. The once quiet flight deck sprung to life with the beeps and bongs of alerts and warnings.

A severe hydraulic leak indication revealed itself and led to system loss coupled with multiple accompanying malfunctions.

The failure caused a manual reversion of the flight controls, making the autopilot disengage. The aircraft felt sluggish and cumbersome without hydraulically assisted steering. *No big deal*, I thought. *I can take my time since I've got plenty of fuel, and we're not on fire.*

"Gabe, I've got the airplane. Declare an emergency and get a vector so we can run some checklists," I said.

"Aviate, navigate, communicate" are three words every pilot knows as the essential internal dialogue during nearly any emergency. "Aviate" directs us to fly the airplane. Countless accidents have resulted in over-fixation of the malfunction. An Eastern Airlines jet tragically crashed into the Everglades years ago as four pilots focused on a faulty landing gear lightbulb. "Navigate" regards maintaining awareness of where the aircraft is going. "Communicate" refers to speaking to those pertinent to that phase of the emergency and muting those who are not.

"American 485, declaring an emergency. We need a heading," Gabe parroted.

"Roger American 485. Understand you are an emergency aircraft. Fly heading 270, maintain 3000 feet."

He read back the clearance given by the check pilot, who played a dual role as Air Traffic Control. A list of tasks followed, necessitating minimal distraction.

"American 485, state the nature of your emergency," ATC interrupted.

"Hydraulic failure," Gabe answered.

"American 485, I need your fuel quantity in pounds and souls on board. What type of assistance will you be requiring? How long would you like to be vectored? Would you like a different altitude?"

"Stay with me, Gabe. Tell him to stand by," I directed.

The chime of the flight attendant call sounded.

When playing the role of Air Traffic Control, check pilots can put a hook in the water to see if they can lead the captain astray. After declaring an emergency, they'll pretend to be an overly chatty controller who only wants to help. They sound a repeated cabin chime of a panicked flight attendant or contrive distractions that draw the pilot away from their primary flight duties. These hooks are useful. They emulate real-world flight emergencies and aim to increase workload while testing the pilot's priorities and resolve. Focusing on flying the airplane, prioritization, and proper delegation of duties to avoid task saturation remain critical in resolving any crisis.

An inflight emergency isn't always limited to the inoperative system but can expand to the accompanying functions of the aircraft, and what initially appears to be a containable emergency can rapidly devolve if not managed correctly. In the case of a hydraulic failure, implications could include aircraft controllability, landing gear extension, flap extension, nose wheel steering control, braking, or any other hydraulically driven component.

Prioritization, delegation, and situational awareness pulled me toward not majoring in the minors. The big picture appeared to be in focus.

With the situation under control, I needed some room to make it all work.

"Gabe, get us an extended vector to the longest runway possible."

"Only one available," the check pilot chirped over my shoulder. His infamous reputation presented itself as he continued to turn the knife.

"We've got ice accretion," I said to Gabe. "That'll increase the approach speeds and alter our landing distance requirements beyond those already imposed by the mechanical failures. Let's make sure we've got enough pavement to land."

"It'll work," the voice injected behind me, saving Gabe the calculation.

I was forced to fly a non-precision offset approach. An offset approach is not lined up with the runway and requires the pilot to turn the aircraft after visual acquisition to align and land. This can offer challenges in the best of conditions but was now even more difficult due to the slow response of the aircraft.

I again pressed the check pilot for any straight-in ILS approach to any runway, preferably a long one. Though this was a simulator, we were told to handle everything as if in a real-life situation. It would be nearly impossible for such a request to be denied during an actual declared emergency.

After multiple inquiries, the check pilot leaned toward me from his control panel behind us and stiffly said, "This is your only approach and your only runway. This is *all* you have available."

I thought, Roger that, peanut breath; bring it. I want to be a captain, and I'll jump through your fiery hoops to get there, and I won't let your ridiculous version of a checkride stand in my way.

We commenced the approach and soon exited the base of the cloud deck—neither the approach light system nor the runway appeared in the place where I'd anticipated. A set of runway lights illuminated to my distant left. I hadn't expected the runway to be that far offset. Something didn't add up.

"Do you see the runway, Gabe?" I asked.

Gabe opened his mouth to speak but said nothing, appearing confused.

"Ask ATC if the runway lights are on." Gabe did so.

"Oh, yeah. Sorry about that. Here ya go," the check pilot said in a mock tone as the correct set of lights switched on and pierced through the darkness ahead.

He had attempted to lure me to the wrong runway.

"Seriously?" I said, loud enough for him to hear me. I wonder how many pilots he'd gaffed with the underhanded trick. I calmed myself, knowing he held my fate.

I looked over at Gabe, who rolled his eyes in concurrence. I pushed the mushy controls, banking the airplane toward the runway. He'd programmed the simulated airport with a contaminated environment and bumped in a very strong direct crosswind from the upwind side, hoping to cause me to overshoot the aligning turn to the short runway. The data would barely put the airplane within the confines of available landing distance, with no room for error.

I considered it even more ironic after the check pilot had informed me that all other runways were unavailable and closed. I fell for none of it and completed the task, but it did not resemble a realistic scenario.

"Okay, that emergency is over. Set your flaps for takeoff, and let's clean up the switches." The screens ahead blanked and then reappeared, displaying the departure runway ahead of the nose. I had cleared the first hurdle.

Another two hours of relentless badgering ensued. We made a final landing in an emergency, simulating an uncontained fire, resulting in an evacuation. As we finished our final checklist, a muted bell rang outside, signaling the gangplank rejoining the box. Sweat soaked my undershirt. The check pilot leaned toward me from his control panel and stuck out his hand.

"Congratulations, Captain," he said. I'd passed.

I headed back to my bathroom altar to pay gratitude.

During the debrief, I had mixed emotions. A warmth of accomplishment filled me, accompanied by a chill of resentment. He showered me with praise on my performance, but I hinted at the intensive set of parameters he'd set. He shrugged it off, intending to deliver someone the same beating the next time. I bit my tongue on a further elaboration and walked out, holding a temporary pilot certificate with a newly inked type rating.

The following morning, I dumped out a suitcase full of dirty clothes in front of the washing machine, happy to be home. The phone rang, and I picked it up, assuming a friend was calling to see how everything had gone.

"Hello, captain. It's Gareth Tomlinson. I'm the fleet training supervisor on the F100."

"Hi, Captain Tomlinson," I answered, nervous, wondering if I'd done something wrong.

"First of all, congratulations on a successful ride yesterday," he assured me. "I want to talk to you about the details of your check flight."

My training partner had thoroughly debriefed every aspect of the check pilot's overzealous examination standards, including the claimed simulator anomaly. His dissertation had joined a list of others. I verified that these were the same parameters I'd been given. Other than the initial wind shear resulting in his crash, I confirmed the accuracy of every detail.

The check pilot had given me his final checkride. He lost his position and returned to regular line flying due to an excessive failure rate fueled by unrealistic scenarios.

Rick retook his checkride the following day and passed with flying colors. He flew as a safe and proficient captain for the next two decades.

7

WHEN HANDS FLY

PUT UP YOUR DUKES

"If you want to beat up my co-pilot, you'll have to go through me first!" I had the young man by six inches, forty pounds, and the sway of his inebriation would play in my favor. I didn't want to fight, but I also didn't want him to incapacitate a fellow crewmember. The situation took a turn south when a dozen cohorts piled in behind him.

How could I ponder a flight cancellation over an ass-kicking at this moment? It's a captain's duty to stand up for his crew, even if this logistically fell well outside of the playbook.

We weren't in an airplane or even the airport terminal. We stood outside of a college bar in Durham, North Carolina.

Chicago's Boeing 727 International division comprised only a small number of pilots. The limited size of the division meant we flew together frequently, and many of us got to know each other well. We commonly referred to ourselves as a tiny airline within a larger one.

I'd flown with Jake multiple times and described him as likable despite the perpetual dark cloud hanging over his head.

Our most frequent route took us from Chicago O'Hare to Monterrey, Mexico, with nearly 30 hours of layover time. Jake and I sat side by side at the pointy end of the airplane on many of those flights. Beyond being a capable pilot, his natural curiosity and fondness for culture made the extended layovers a reason for him to venture out. I occasionally went along. We'd wander the city streets, and the owners of local establishments often greeted him with handshakes and warm smiles. I nicknamed Jake the "Mayor of Monterrey."

Despite his cordial nature, Jake had knack for finding the sharp end of someone's sword. If lightning struck the same place twice, Jake would be standing there both times. One evening, my lightning rod theory nearly burned us both.

Deviating from our normal international schedule, our flight sequence had been reprogrammed with some domestic legs, finishing the day in Raleigh-Durham, North Carolina. We landed mid-afternoon, looking forward to a 20-hour stay in Durham, before being scheduled back out on a flight the following morning.

We set the brakes, ran through, and completed our shutdown checklist.

"What are your plans for the evening, Jake?"

"Think I'll walk around and check out the area. Wanna come?"

"Yeah, sure," I said. "If I don't leave a crumb trail, I'll get lost anyway."

Remembering Jake's escapades in Mexico, I knew he'd be eager to discover the lay of the land. We met in the hotel lobby and set out but soon became parched with only limited options to quench our thirsts. The layover hotel bordered the Duke University campus, leaving us no choice but to settle for a local college bar.

We stumbled across our best option, entered, and bellied up to a noisy but not ear-piercing locale. College-aged kids populated the establishment with the energy of youth. We didn't fit the demographic, but we'd found cold drinks.

The noise level rose steadily as more young patrons rolled in, impeding normal conversation—time to backtrack to the hotel. Now densely crowded, the congestion made navigation toward an exit a challenge.

While sliding between bodies, Jake bumped the elbow of a girl holding a cocktail, spilling the drink. Unaware of his actions, he continued to fumble toward the door, only to be followed by the disgruntled young lady and her date.

Once outside, the girl rounded on Jake and hurled the rest of her cocktail into his face.

In a misdirected act of chivalry, her stout young date had followed behind, deciding to take it to the next level. He wound back to deliver a barrage of punches. The first swing grazed Jake's nose. Alcohol had contributed to his miscalculation, but he'd undoubtedly land a shot at this range soon.

"You're dead, old man!" barked the kid.

I wedged between them, pushing the aggressor back with more force than he'd anticipated. He regained his balance, paused, aware of my presence, and studied my frame with foggy trepidation. He contemplated his next move, eyeing a more formidable opponent while not wanting to lose face with his date. Reinforcements arrived within seconds as his cohorts poured out of the bar. I'd met the Duke Lacrosse Team on the wrong terms.

My intercedence had bought us a few seconds as the kid, aware of a significant regained advantage, said," Both of you are going to take a beating."

I took a defensive stance and replied, "Probably, but I'll get a few shots in on you before I hit the ground."

He wavered, juggling the possibility of impending personal injury. A teammate chimed in and chirped up from behind him, hurling insults at Jake's attire. I'd have to concede to the accuracy, considering pilots are not the best dressers and, when out of uniform, are often easily identified by their taste in clothing.

I looked back at the young man who'd commented and noticed a striking resemblance to Paul Reubens, aka Pee Wee Herman. Reubens, a famous comic, had recently had a run-in with the law that had gained national attention after he exposed himself at an adult theatre.

I changed tack, calling the guy "Pee Wee Herman's evil twin" while questioning his affinity to also take part in exposure and self-pleasure in public places.

The stab hit home, and a collective chuckle rose from the Duke Lacrosse Team. I'd found the black sheep of their clan and scored a direct hit. It's hard to fight someone when they're making you laugh.

"Guys, let's go inside, and I'll buy you all a beer," I offered.

"Really? Sure," one quickly accepted.

We went back inside, and everyone quickly forgave each other. They ended up being decent kids, albeit a rowdy bunch. Having no idea what prompted the ruckus, they'd run outside to stand up for their crew the same way I'd stood up for mine in the spirit of "shoot first and ask questions later."

We parted with handshakes and fist bumps.

Jake's head hung low on the walk back to the hotel, the perpetual dark cloud still hovering above. We shared a nervous laugh, knowing we'd out-maneuvered a less desirable outcome with little more than quick wit.

The following morning, our crew loaded onto the van and headed to the airport.

"What did you all do yesterday?" inquired a flight attendant.

"Just took a stroll," I answered.

I shot Jake a grin. Some part of "We almost got our asses kicked in a college bar" remained best unsaid.

Years later, Jake thanked me for standing up for him that day. I don't know if my reaction had been the brightest idea, but we'd luckily escaped what could have been an undeserved, and likely painful, beating.

8

NOSEDIVE

NOT DOING AS YOU'RE TOLD.

"Don't disconnect the autopilot! If you miss the approach, you need to keep it engaged. I'm going to put you back to the outer marker so that you can do it again."

The simulator instructor had a frustrated edge in his voice, knowing we'd have to redo the approach and go-around procedure. The displays blanked, and instruments spun backward as the sim dialed back to an earlier stage of the approach procedure. The instructor continued elaborating, hoping my trigger finger wouldn't press the autopilot disengage button again.

"Captain, it's a critical phase of flight, and with the airplane trimmed to land, you don't want to disengage the autopilot that close to the ground if you go around. If you don't see the runway at decision height, push the throttles forward and bring your hand back to the autopilot control knob, pulling it aft to pitch the nose up," he finished.

"Cooperate and graduate," I whispered.

The instructor placed his right hand over the throttles and then brought them back to the cap-shaped knob of the autopilot control to mimic the motion. "Like this, see?"

"Gotta let George fly it," I said, winking at my sim partner.

Autopilots, often referred to as "George" back in the day, could have minds of their own. They had a basic three-axis function and sometimes a problematic coupling to the navigation system. Without the multiple redundancy of today's autopilots, the words, "What are you doing now, George?" commonly rang across the flight deck. Sometimes, the altitude hold mode didn't work, or the aircraft would wander. It made me all the wearier of letting George fly an approach to within one hundred feet of the ground.

The instructor zeroed the visibility of the forward projection screens, assuring that there'd be no way I'd see the runway or runway environment, prompting the missed approach go-around.

This time, I followed the instructions when reaching our decision height of one hundred feet above the ground. The simulator complied, its nose pointing toward the obscured sky to the beat of a trim wheel clicking aft as we reconfigured flaps and landing gear for the maneuver.

"Much better," he complimented.

Yup, cooperate and graduate, I concluded, but it felt unnatural and counterintuitive. Training my motor skills away from disengaging the autopilot pushed against thousands of hours of muscle memory and twenty years of flying instinct. Within several months, the contest of procedures versus my instincts would be tested in the real world.

★★★

From backyard barbeques to wedding receptions, when someone learns I'm a pilot, I can bank on a few inevitable questions.

The first is, "What's your route?"

The answer is easy. If my division qualifications are up to date, it's anywhere the airplane can be scheduled to fly. If I'm not in the mood to elaborate, I'll name a city and call it good.

The second question is, "Do you know Mike? Maybe it's Mark. He flies fishing charters somewhere out of Alaska, or maybe it's Cape Cod." Although the answer is nearly always no, I once answered yes on the way home from the airport in Miami. While pumping gas, someone noticed my pilot shirt and asked about a New York-based pilot who happened to be a guy I'd recently flown with. File it into the category of finding a needle in a haystack.

Question three asks, "Have you ever had a serious emergency or almost crashed?" Most fellow pilots luckily answer "No." My answer to that one is "Yes." It's not a fun story, but it ended well.

By the late-1990s, I'd advanced to the captain's seat of the Boeing 727. Now thirty-four years old, I'd gotten to know the airplane well, having been a flight engineer and flown it as first officer. The jet delivered a heavy yet predictable feel while pummeling the egos of even the best pilots. You could land perfectly nine times only to slap the runway on the tenth landing. If the airplane could laugh, it probably would, having force-fed you a slice of humble pie.

★★★

On a murky Missouri morning, I passed through the security area to board the airplane. Family members wished their loved ones a safe journey outside the gate area. Kansas City airport had a different setup back then. Each gate had a security screener, and people could say goodbye to their loved ones outside the boarding area. Though inefficient, this system had its benefits.

I noticed a teary-eyed woman hugging her college-aged daughter, not wanting to let her go. It reminded me that her life and the lives of all the other passengers had been entrusted to me. *Don't worry, Mom*, I thought; *I'll get her there safely.*

Despite the short distance between Kansas City airport and Chicago O'Hare, I added plenty of extra fuel due to deteriorating weather conditions in Chicago. Shortly after our wheels left the runway from Kansas City, Chicago O'Hare weather had become duck soup.

The low visibility approach I'd practiced at the Schoolhouse a few months earlier was about to be tested.

Aircraft piled into holding patterns as they approached O'Hare, to soon be vectored, slotted, and spaced for the low visibility approaches. Our flight crew briefed the procedure in detail, including a refresher on appropriate callouts and the missed approach procedure.

Airplanes lined up like Rockettes on a chorus line to navigate through the bleak day, hoping to breakout beneath the low hanging clouds and land. When it came to our turn, we lined up for a long final approach, intercepted the Instrument Landing System for our final descent to the runway, and commenced the approach. With the single-channel autopilot engaged, the airplane captured the runway 14R glideslope.

FLYING AND DYING

The approach continued normally as the airliner ahead of us reported clearing the runway, a required call with the control tower unable to see the aircraft.

"Roger United 485, contact ground 121.9. Before you switch, where did you break out?"

"Point 9, and we broke out right at minimums," he answered.

We made the next required callout of altitude above the ground, airspeed deviation, and rate of descent.

"500, on speed, sink 750."

Locked and loaded in the final stages of the approach, the procedure required me to direct my primary attention outside to pick out the approach lights, runway, or runway environment as the first officer continued monitoring the instruments for any deviation.

I scanned through the windshield into an abyss of thick gray fog, knowing the runway threshold awaited on the other side.

At about 250 feet above the ground, I felt a subtle bump as my hands guarded the flight controls. It caused me to look back inside (another thing I wasn't supposed to do). The airplane had made a slight pull to correct back to the glide slope, having come slightly off its path but not enough to warrant a deviation callout.

Though minimal, the bump felt strangely out of place.

Rather than reattain the path, the autopilot correction had caused the aircraft to start losing the top of the glide path, at which point all hell broke loose. The autopilot dove the airplane into a severe pitch-over so significant that it nearly pulled the controls from my hands.

"Go around, go around!" I shouted.

My trigger finger didn't care what I'd been taught in the simulator as I disconnected the autopilot and reefed back on the controls while advancing the throttles. To this day, it's the hardest I've ever pulled on a commercial aircraft - the G-force was certainly felt by everyone in the airplane. The airplane complied and changed direction, barely missing the approach light system.

We initially considered that faulty ground equipment might have driven the event or theorized an interruption of a correct glideslope signal. We attempted a second approach to a higher approach criterion but couldn't exit the cloud base. We diverted to Indianapolis and waited until the Chicago weather lifted.

Pilots learn to reduce levels of technology in critical situations. Automation dependency has led to numerous problems.

My issue stemmed from reliance on a single-channel autopilot as the means of control during such a critical phase of flight. Replacing the pilot with a non-redundant archaic technology pushed against instinct, learning, and common sense.

I debriefed the event, entitling the report "CAT 2 Nosedive", referring to the Category 2 approach procedure. I called our union safety chairman and the company fleet manager.

"We believe it was a rare, singular event," the safety chairman concluded.

I followed up with the aircraft fleet manager.

"The Boeing 727 is programmed to enter a pitch desensitization mode over ninety seconds after capturing the glideslope," he explained. "It happens internally without any flight deck indication. It keeps the airplane from getting excessive nose-up or nose-down inputs from the autopilot once you're near the ground."

"We changed a faulty pitch channel on the airplane," he continued. "Your incident was isolated, and we don't think it'll happen again."

Less than two months later, another Boeing 727 flew the exact route from Kansas City to Chicago O'Hare. When landing on Runway 14R in low visibility conditions, it encountered the same pitch-over, resulting in a complete hull loss of the airplane.

Captain Chuck Valle had also instinctively uncoupled the autopilot and pulled back on the controls. Unable to arrest the excessive sink rate, the aircraft hit the ground just over 300 feet from the end of the runway, shearing off the landing gear and heavily damaging the fuselage and wings. It slid through the dirt to the right of the runway where it came to a stop. Thankfully, Captain Valle's skill averted the loss of life. They initially attempted to point to pilot error until they came across my incident report.

The next call came from the NTSB. At a subsequent hearing, I testified to the events of that day. My testimony cleared Captain Valle and his crew of any wrongdoing, though the outcome still had an unclear conclusion. Back at the Flight Academy, a new simulator training procedure was added to address the pitch-over event.

I attended a captains duties and responsibilities gathering not long after. The combined training and celebration taught new captains the nuances of their roles as captains. It culminated with a dinner with flight management and a personalized plaque. They'd been running behind on this class as I'd already been a captain for over three years, now in command of my second airplane.

Our then Vice President of Flight, Captain Cecil Ewell, attended the dinner. He was among the most beloved, regarded, and respected pilot advocates the airline had ever known. He bridged the gap between an adverse management and sometimes rebellious pilot group. His reasonable perspective and an endearing southern drawl drew the respect of the most temperamental pilots when upper management maintained an aggressive leadership style.

Captain Ewell spoke.

"I want to tell you about one of my first trips on the Airbus A300," he began. "The leg took us overwater from New York to San Juan. Things were going just fine until we recorded a position report and noticed the fuel was several thousand pounds below our anticipated quantity. We had a severe fuel leak and had no idea how to stop it. Fuel was gushing out of the wing tank, and if we didn't do something quickly, both engines would cease due to fuel starvation.

"Nothing worked, and at the rate we were losing fuel, we wouldn't be able to get to a diversion airport. Once we ran dry, we would have to ditch into the sea, so we briefed for a water landing, knowing the engines would soon flame out. As we called our mayday over the emergency frequency of the radio, the voice of a pilot from a nearby aircraft replied.

"Pull the fire handle for the engine on the side of your leak!" he said. "As it turned out, the pilot had substantial experience on the Airbus."

"With nothing else to lose, we did so, knowing it would flame out the engine on that side. Pulling the fire handle closed fuel shutoffs at the engine and back at the tank, stopping the leak."

"We hobbled to the enroute alternate on the other engine and landed with only minutes of fuel remaining. The airplane barely had enough gas to taxi to the gate," Captain Ewell said, reliving the moment.

"During our careers, in tens of thousands of hours, we may only have one instance when the experience we've accumulated results in saving an aircraft. We need to be ready when it does."

He walked to my table and put his arm around my shoulder.

"This guy knows exactly what that means. He's already seen that instance and saved an airplane with over 150 lives aboard."

Captain Ewell's validation meant a lot and helped me move forward.

Captain Sully Sullenberger commanded a forced water landing on the Hudson River in 2009. He stated in an interview, "One way of looking at this might be that, for forty-two years, I've been making deposits in this bank of experience. And on January 15, the balance was sufficient so that I could make a very large withdrawal."

I'd also made a withdrawal from my bank of experience. And contrary to what I had been trained to do, my actions resulted in a favorable outcome.

During the moments of my nosedive, other than being pushed into their seats during the pull-up, passengers never knew how close they'd come to making the newspapers. My thoughts returned to the mother in Kansas City, not wanting to let go of her daughter. My heart filled with gratitude, knowing I'd kept her safe.

9

THE AMBASSADOR

SMILES EVERYBODY, SMILES

With over 3000 daily flights, things don't always go as planned.

I've always tried to advocate for and validate others, especially those who put food on my table. As an airline pilot, fulfilling my job description can manifest a unique shape, and the expression of professionalism transforms that role.

Many pilots contend that their job is the operation of the aircraft, but our leadership role extends beyond the wingspan, making it essential to wear other hats when necessary. Diplomacy intertwines with countless facets of our occupation.

When a passenger gets on my airplane, they matter. One of the central tenets of this book is to be kind to others. Its application in my chosen field reverberates at many levels.

Some years back, as a captain on the Boeing 757, I sat at the flight deck preparing the aircraft for departure at the San Francisco International Airport.

After his exterior preflight, the first officer entered the flight deck, letting out an audible sigh.

"Hey Cap, you're not gonna like this," he opened.

"Uh oh, what's up?"

"We've got a good bit of hydraulic fluid around the right main landing gear."

"Any chance it's from a previous airplane or servicing?"

"Doesn't look that way," he said.

"Okay, let's give maintenance a call, and I'll go have a look."

I clanged down the metal jet bridge stairs, hoping I might find some residual spill from an overfilled reservoir—no such luck. The brake lines around the landing gear dripped fluid in a puddle, advancing around the wheel assemblies.

"Arg, we're not going anywhere," I mumbled, knowing this would take the aircraft out of service.

Once the engines started and engine hydraulic pumps came online, the acceleration of pressure would quickly have lowered or even emptied the hydraulic reservoir. The preflight inspection had fortunately alerted us.

I contemplated a proactive game plan as I trotted back up the jet bridge stairs. Rather than wait for multiple protocols leading to the inevitable, I hurried along the jet bridge to involve the gate agent.

"All set?" she said suspiciously.

"Yeah, about that…"

Coincidentally, an earlier delayed flight, parked at an adjacent gate, was now only a few minutes from being buttoned up and on its way. After a couple quick phone calls, the gate agent quickly began coordinating and rebooking as many passengers as possible to maintain the continuity of those with connections.

Before their disembarking, I made a PA to share the news. As the passengers collected their belongings and filed off the airplane, I stood at the door to wish them well despite the unforeseen circumstances. I couldn't help but smile triumphantly, having been a steward of my profession beyond its normal description.

One gentleman scampered up the aisle, looking at me with a crooked mouth and hateful eyes. He stopped, narrowed his gaze, and snapped, "Lies, lies, lies! I hate this airline!"

He derailed my happy train.

"Buh-bye, have a nice day," I offered, pushing up the sides of my mouth into a forced grin.

As an ambassador of my occupation, I realized there would be those who don't trust us, but it didn't stop me from doing my best. That day, I stepped outside my job description and took a verbal lashing from an ungracious passenger. I'd do the same thing if I had to do it again.

With hundreds of passengers on board, I cannot assume that each is headed to a white sandy beach, swimming pool, or a tiki bar.

Some are going to important meetings and interviews and have scheduled the events of their day based on the assumption of an on-time arrival. To others, timely arrival is of critical importance. Some will see loved ones, maybe for the last time. Some are going to funerals or to be near someone who desperately needs them.

Though the safety of the aircraft is the first order of business, my title as a captain is that of a leader. It has been said many times that we don't know what any person is going through at any moment. From a nervous passenger who looks to me for my sobriety and professional intention to the million-plus mile frequent flyer whose daily flights are as common as driving their car, my good intention, my demeanor, and my heartfelt commitment to them carry the purpose of my profession.

★★★

Crew members often sit in the back of an aircraft, whether deadheading to a trip segment or commuting to or from work. Traveling in the passenger cabin while in uniform inevitably triggers one universal statement.

"Shouldn't you be in the front of the airplane?"

"Not at all. I can fly it from back here using my iPad."

The part of me that enjoys humorous exchanges with passengers persists. The conversations become funny and inquisitive, especially when something is afoot.

Eyes will shoot in my direction when the aircraft hits turbulence, is delayed, or encounters a mechanical problem. On a recent flight, the captain came on the PA to inform the passengers that the plane had been taken out of service.

Maintenance had come aboard, and after about 15 minutes, the passengers were asked to disembark. Fortunately, another aircraft could accommodate these folks, and the leg was not canceled. Despite the good news, the passengers were frustrated as there was no clear explanation for the sudden equipment change.

On the way out, I leaned into the flight deck as the aircraft disembarked, curious about why the plane was being taken out of service.

"Hey, Captain. What'd you break?" I opened kiddingly.

"It wasn't me," he said, smiling. "Apparently, this thing is an oil burner. Maintenance is taking it to the hangar."

"How bad?"

"They've had to add oil every leg. The last leg was excessive, so this thing is dead in the water."

"Good call," I said. He'd taken a low-key approach in the elaboration of his passenger announcement. Different captains run the ship in different ways, and he'd chosen the most conservative path.

No matter what the airline or the plane, an issue of this sort is a legitimate reason for removing the equipment from regular service. It's essential to speak the truth, but it's equally important to tread carefully.

Some would rightfully question giving the passengers too much detail. I believe they deserve to hear the truth, always considering the thickness of that slice. In this case, it walks a fine line of disclosure.

Most of the passengers would have been appeased to know that the airline was taking a proactive approach toward the maintenance of this aircraft, heading off a potentially more severe maintenance issue. It's a matter of packaging.

You be the captain and choose the announcement.

"Hi folks, this airplane is being taken out of service because…"

1. "We have a maintenance issue."

2. "Maintenance has alerted us to some negative mechanical trending, and they need to assess the issue."

3. "The right engine has been trending higher than normal oil burn, and mechanics want to have a closer look."

4. "The right engine has been burning an excessive amount

of oil, increasing its potential of failure in flight."

"We have another airplane available at a different gate."

All these announcements add to the same result, and the bad news / good news element beats a cancelation anytime. Most captains will defer the first or second choice for sound reasons. A seasoned passenger might only feel concerned with the last announcement, whereas a fearful passenger might be terrified by any of them. A need exists to cater to the most fearful passengers, like a restaurant caters to the weakest customer's food sensitivity.

I overhear a passenger conversation and can identify the veteran flyer. A patient woman packs away her laptop computer.

"Can you believe we have to walk all the way to another gate?" one chides.

"They have a spare airplane, the flight is going, and you're going to Grand Rapids instead of a hotel here for the night," she reassures them.

I smile and acknowledge the passenger, grateful for veteran flyers who settle the less experienced ones. Words matter.

10

Help Wanted

The Peacekeeper

First Officer Greg Skeens cackled with annoyance. In another realm, his rank drew intimidation, but that position didn't hold power or authority in this corner of the civilian world. Here, he wore a different hat.

"I like to be in command. I spent thousands of hours in the left seats of military jets and was a captain back at the regionals," he barked.

"I respect your experience, Greg, and you can spend thousands more when you upgrade to captain here. You're a strong resource to the flight deck, but certain decisions fall outside your purview. You need to maintain your role as a first officer," I responded. I remained calm but wasn't backing down.

"I understand," Greg relented. "I'll back off."

One of the most heartwarming, heartbreaking, and entertaining elements of my flying career didn't involve flying. It involved the intervention, perspective, problem-solving, and peacekeeping of my Pilot Professional Standards Committee tenure.

This call had a common theme. In a cyclical airline industry, stagnating advancement led to frustration, and highly skilled pilots ready to take command acted out frustrations from the right seat. A pilot with a high military ranking or substantial pilot-in-command time at a previous occupation transitioned to the bottom of the list in their new career. Entry-level positions don't exist at large US carriers; promotion is seniority-based. My new job served our union in a peer support and resolution function. The need to give something back to the occupation I loved had led me here.

I searched for the right fit to involve myself in a committee. Safety, Training, and Family Awareness all had an appeal, but Pilot Professional Standards stood out.

The skills I'd gained as a police officer lent themselves to the flight deck. Strong and stubborn personalities could clash in the tiny space in the front of the airplane, requiring tactful intervention.

The balance of the conflict involved calling back the captain and assuring everyone had learned something and could move forward.

"Hi Captain, It's Tom from Pro Standards."

"Did you put him in his place?"

"Slow down. You and I need to debrief this, too," I shot back. "This isn't about making anyone a punching bag."

"So, what's up?" he continued, not realizing we also had a few things to talk about.

"I've heard both sides. Yes, Greg needs to regard you and the decisions you make as the captain, but you need to act like one. Pointing at the four stripes on your jacket isn't the way to command respect. Lead by example. He's a well-qualified pilot, an essential resource, and the person who'll keep you out of trouble. The only license he has to lose - is yours. So, treat him with respect."

"Yeah, well, okay." He sat silently with my words, not expecting to get an earful.

I softened my tone. "Let's learn from this and put it behind us," I closed.

This call was one of the first of hundreds I'd handle.

The Chicago domicile committee was comprised of only a few pilots with a limited but essential task. In the late '90s, the influence of the committee had limitations. Although regarded for its successful flight deck interventions, the tiger had yet to cut its teeth. As described by the name, we voluntarily oversaw the adherence to professionalism. That definition could cast a broad net as Pilot Professional Standards reps had a knack for confronting and resolving issues inherent to the dynamics of pilot personalities.

Training didn't exist for the committee back then, so I figured it out as I went, using common sense and problem-solving skills. The union gave us autonomy, and the flight office happily allowed us to shorten the stack of paper that would have otherwise landed on their desks.

We'd hear the problem, get all sides, make recommendations, or impose solutions, burn the paperwork, and claim 100% amnesia if anyone ever asked about it.

I could resolve some issues with a quick phone call and some healthy perspective. Other incidents had more layers than a wedding cake. They could involve multiple workgroups with emotional, if not high-conflict, personalities. They'd necessitate the balance of a high-wire act while walking a tightrope of potential career or life-altering consequences.

Domicile Pro Standards committees balanced their members to delegate cases to the closest peer. We'd pair a senior captain having an issue with a senior pilot committee member rather than a junior first officer. We matched a more aggressive pilot with a more in-your-face committee member. It yielded the greatest likelihood of a positive outcome.

The Pilot Professional Standards Committees had an admirably high percentage of resolving issues thanks to its members' diversity and the union hierarchy's support. Certain pilots drove our workload more than others. We referred to them as "Frequent Flyers" and joked that 95 percent of our work came from the same 5 percent of the pilot group.

When the phone rang, I could be confident of one thing - for the next several minutes, the voice on the other side would fill my ears with anything from an anecdotal vent to a life-altering saga. I had to be ready for either.

11

DIFFERENT FEATHERS

GETTING ALONG WITH OTHERS

Birds of a feather don't always fly together. The flight deck's oil and water standard is called the "do-not-pair" list. These are pilots who feel their personality conflict could impair safety. Some captains have impressively long lists of pilots who won't fly with them, to the point that they need to change domiciles to find a fresh crop of crew members who hopefully will.

Pilot Professional Standards wasn't beyond going toe to toe with these folks, having the liberty to speak our minds unfiltered. Involvement in cases predicated a mutual voluntary participation agreement, allowing dialogues to evolve organically. The "between you and me" format allowed conversations to take directions that would otherwise be unheard of or illegal. We could be candid.

"You've got quite a do-not-pair list. Can we talk about that?"

"Been flying with a lot of boneheads lately. They can't handle my leadership style."

"Sounds like your leadership style is pretty aggressive, captain."

"If they don't like it, they don't have to fly with me," he snapped.

The conversation could take one of two directions from here. Some dug their heels in, showing why nearly no one wanted to fly with them. Others were baffled, lacking social cues, and saw themselves differently.

Rather than continue down that alley, I needed to take a different angle. If I asked the right questions, I could control the direction of the dialogue. I spoke the following words solemnly, summoning them from a compassionate corner of my heart.

"How's everything going at home, Sam?"

He paused, sensing genuine concern in my voice. An unspoken trust between pilots held the new moment.

"Rough patch. My wife doesn't understand the job." A slight tremble impinged his bravado.

"Your home address is Chicago, but you're New York-based. Why aren't you Chicago-based?"

The New York crew base had always been the most junior, allowing quick upgrades to larger aircraft or captain's seats, but the promotions came at a price. I knew the answer before he shaped the words.

"Chicago? It's senior, and I can't hold captain there," he said, returning to his egoic edge. "I'd have to go back to co-pilot."

"Yeah, but you can hold your family there. Sitting in a Jackson Heights commuter pad waiting for the phone to ring costs you a lot of your life. Every dime is worth about five cents in a divorce."

Our conversation revealed a direction airline management couldn't take under labor laws, no matter how genuine the intention. As Pro Standards reps, the pilots we spoke to agreed to allow this breadth of dialogue, having decided to consider our perspective as peers. The pilots we talked to could tell us it was none of our concern, but they also understood we served as advocates, many of whom weathered similar storms.

"I've got bills. You know what a GX-470 runs these days?" he countered, revealing his edge.

"It's better to be in Chicago with your family loading them into a Toyota than sitting on call in New York while your spouse loads them into a Lexus. Just sayin'."

I'd held my ground and made my point, knowing he'd have a few things to chew on. I also learned not to go beyond pointing out those simple truths. Speaking to his previous first officers revealed him to be a safe but short-fused pilot. Our job was to seek cause rather than treat effect.

"You've got my number. Call me anytime, 24/7," I closed.

This pilot, like many others, had a choice to make. Knowing the most important part of your job is the family you come home to is a foregone conclusion to some, a painful jolt of reality for others. The accommodation of that reality would result in an amenable or embattled crewmember.

A day later, Sam called to continue our conversation, starting where we had left off.

"I don't want to be that guy," he opened. "That's the guy on the bathroom walls of ops. The one no one will fly with."

"We all hit bumps along the way," I reassured him. "My best advice is to get your life squared away at home. When things are rough at the homestead, you can't expect them to go well at work. It's that whole life balance thing."

"I see your point," he admitted. "I've been a little edgy and distracted."

"Pilots, flight attendants, and anyone else you work with are your greatest allies. They've got your back if you've got theirs. If you regard them well, they'll go to bat for you. When I finish a trip, I always thank everyone for keeping me out of trouble. We're human, we make mistakes, and we can capture each other's errors. If you negate your resources, you've impaired safety."

I knew I'd given Sam a sermon, but he needed to hear it. He'd become too much of a one-man show, and his decision to open his ears invited a healthy reality check. Like our conversation the day before, I gave him enough to chew on, but not too much.

The pilot ego can obscure safe operation of the aircraft. When a captain believes he needs to micromanage each detail of the operation either out of authority or paranoia, they can lose sight of the big picture. Sam had begun to lose sight of the big picture, and Pro Standard's task was to refocus the lens.

I finished the conversation with a Goethe quote I've used for years. "Don't let the things that matter most be at the mercy of the things that matter least."

"Gotcha," he said with a touch of resignation in his voice. My words had settled in with him, considering the direction I'd suggested.

Sam transferred back to Chicago to be with his family, albeit as an international widebody first officer. The once empty lawn chair at the sidelines of his kid's soccer games was now occupied by a husband and a father who cheered his family.

12

HELP NEEDED

PILOT ASSISTANCE EVOLVES

I nudged my first officer, noticing his mind was wandering.

"Scott, you need to start down for us to comply with that next crossing restriction ahead."

"Oh yeah, here we go," he said as he snapped back into his role and engaged the aircraft's descent mode. The thrust levers pulled back toward the stops as the nose lowered. Alerted by my reminder, Scott realized he'd selected the mode slightly too late and would need to deploy some speed brake to meet the next assigned altitude and speed.

I considered that I'd been trapping a higher-than-normal number of his errors. He'd missed several radio calls and other routine items on the previous leg.

"Oh, sorry," he'd say each time.

"That's why there are two of us up here," I'd answer, a cliche that rings throughout flight decks worldwide.

He continued to drift from the tasks at hand.

I'd tried conversing with Scott several times, but he kept his distance. Our chats were chopped and distracted. His thoughts continually drifted him to a different place.

I had to say something, so I spoke up.

"You all right, buddy?"

He looked up with annoyance as if hoping to capture a conveyance from above, then audibly exhaled as he again looked forward, making a silent admission to my awareness of his state of mind.

"Yeah, I'm good," he said. His words barely carried to my side of the flight deck.

I'd flown with Scott before; our previous trip was a day-turn to Miami and back. On that trip, he had an engaging and charismatic personality. Beyond his flying career, he flew his own airplane on days off, a passionate aviator with razor-sharp flying skills. People who flew with him noticed his proficiency and personality. Scott's quick and contagious smile pulled others toward his positivity. Many at the Chicago crew base knew and regarded him for organizing crew events involving local entertainment.

On this day, he wasn't the same person I'd flown with previously. Something had gotten under his skin.

"Are you sure, Scott?" I said with assertion.

"Yeah. Actually, no," he admitted. "I've got some family issues, and my head is pretty messed up. I think I might need to get off this trip."

His pain filled the flight deck, and I sat helpless to assist. The poor guy was suffering, and I didn't know what to do. How could I help him? We both knew he didn't belong on the flight deck of an airliner, but I felt helpless and inept in rendering any assistance. We sent a message to take Scott off the trip when we landed in Chicago. Another pilot finished the sequence, but the weight of not knowing or directing Scott toward helpful resources left me feeling empty.

After the trip, I talked to some friends who worked at the airline.

"There's not much help for stuff like that," they'd say.

"Why not? Isn't the mental health of pilots critical?"

"It is, but passengers don't want a depressed pilot flying the airplane," they'd answer regretfully.

Scott took his own life a month later, leaving behind a wife, children, family, and friends devastated by his loss and the hole left in their lives. At his service, we shared a deep hurt. He wasn't the only one. Too many pilots with nowhere to turn resorted to extreme measures to stop their pain. Airline pilot suicide rates climbed as we stood by without legitimate resources to quell the issue.

A change had to come from the top.

When a fellow pilot is missing more than they would typically miss, it could be a subtle signal of a deeper underlying issue. A pilot's mind could drift into a dark corner unseen to others.

It may be a distraction or oversight of what may be considered a simple, manageable, and capturable error. Many of these oversights could be attributed to fatigue or any other number of other contributing factors. None of them by themselves would be considered suspicious or dangerous.

One of the most important lessons I learned as a Professional Standards representative was to be acutely aware of the subtle clues of a fellow crewmember in a state of decline.

It emphasized the importance of initiating dialogue between crew members. Sometimes, it was difficult for a pilot to ascertain the actual state of the person they were flying with. A non-consequential interaction became vital in making pilots more forthright with what's going on in their lives.

Other airlines had similar plights. I attended an ALPA (Airline Pilots Association) conference to learn from the stories of other Pilot Assistance volunteers. Many shared a common thread.

"We took a call from a Captain recently," he said. "His first officer was distant and barely spoke. For the first day or so, he was stone-faced and stoic. Out of nowhere, he burst into tears, sobbing uncontrollably. His son had died suddenly, the result of a violent crime. He attended services on his days off and then returned to the flight deck without ever taking the time to heal or seek help."

"We need to do better," he said, scanning the room. "We need to tighten the net, so people don't fall through it. It's on us to educate other crew members to become more adept at the signs of distress or depression."

With the overwhelming support of both the Allied Pilots Association and American Airlines, it became our unrelenting goal to support pilots in need.

13

STEPPING UP

THE NATIONAL COMMITTEE

The caller ID displayed a Fort Worth, Texas, area code. Since Ft. Worth was the headquarters for American Airlines and the Allied Pilots Association, I concluded it had to be work or union related. I hadn't dinged any airplane wingtips or broken any flight regulations. Nothing exceptional that could warrant a call, anyway, so I answered.

"Hey Tom, it's Tom Ray with Pilot Pro Standards National." Yeah, we're both named Tom.

He'd been delegated the new chairman of our national committee.

"I really like your Boeing 757/767 Study Guide," he opened. "It always helps me get through recurrent training."

"Aw, thanks. I wrote it because I have to explain the systems to myself in a way that I can understand them. Once I break something down to its simplest form, I can wrap my brain around it."

Pilots occasionally called, hoping I'd send them a free guide. *Dude, they're only twenty bucks, and that barely covers printing costs. Go buy one at the Flight Academy*, I thought.

When learning a new airplane, I'd supplemented each ground school course by writing my own training material that explained systems and components in a "For Dummies" manner. It entailed everything from flowcharts illustrating how aircraft systems interact to acronyms that helped me remember critical components. Fellow pilots asked for the notes, and I began producing them as study guides. They became popular, and several thousand sold within the airline, giving me a degree of in-house micro fame.

Once, during recurrent training, I sat with my first officer in a briefing room, being given a systems oral exam by a company check pilot. I was crushing it until the first officer spoke up and said, "Did you know Tom writes a study guide on the airplane?"

The check pilot paused, looked at me a bit baffled, and said, "That's you? I get a lot of my ideas for exam questions from that guide."

A short time later, in the breakroom, I overhead the check pilot laughingly saying to someone, "I just gave a pilot a test from his own book!"

Someone would occasionally ask me to sign a copy. I'd sign it – "*insert name*, thanks for teaching me everything in this guide – I couldn't have written it without you. Captain Tom." If someone wanted an autographed copy, I wanted to give them a flex in return.

The notoriety was appealing, but my motive for writing the guide was to get me through training. Apparently, the guide had drawn the interest of the new national Professional Standards chairman.

"Any chance you could write some guidance for our committee? We could move you up to the national level," Tom offered.

"Yeah, sure," I answered, envisioning a different motive.

The quick yes didn't attach to my desire to write another guide. I'd have preferred a root canal. Instead, I had an ulterior motive: getting my foot in the door.

The call was the first step to gaining the involvement I wanted at all committee levels. After over a decade of domicile work, I envisioned the leverage at the national level to push a campaign to fill a sizeable gap.

The change I longed to see stemmed from calls I'd received over the years and held a commonality of foundational issues. Pilots in conflicts at work often had problems away from work. Conversations unfolded with striking similarity.

It's difficult for pilots to be a part of normal society due to the inherent characteristics of their jobs. They're often gone on weekends, transport passengers during the holidays, or work odd hours that alter normal circadian rhythm. When they're home, they may be sleeping or recovering, while those with normal circadian rhythms embark upon their normal days.

Pilots, especially those of lower seniority, can't participate in bowling leagues, softball teams, or other social activities – at least not consistently, due to the demands of their schedules.

We can better understand people in the way we feel them within ourselves. Some of the most successful pilot assistance volunteers stand atop mountains they climbed from the depths of their own despair. I understood a reclusive and disconnected element could contribute to stress at home and the decay of mental health that goes with it. Few are immune to this, and I had once danced with depression.

I'd swallowed a serious dose of my own medicine after my divorce. Cold, dank Michigan winters had left me in a dark place—fifty shades of gray painted the skies and my heart. My solution was to become a first officer, following the advice I'd often given to others. After twenty years as a captain, I'd temporarily bid back to the right seat of a widebody to hold a better schedule. The mindset stung, but the rewards of a wide-open flight schedule soon followed.

I'd go to San Diego on days free of other commitments, where I learned to surf. The salty cold of morning waves slapped a new reality into my world. Afterward, I'd sit at the Bird Rock Coffee Shop, sometimes for hours, and allow a shutdown and caffeine reboot of my mind to renew and refresh my perspective. The sound of friendly chatter, organic choices, ubiquitous gyms and yoga studios, and an amenable climate re-sculpted me.

Progress at the national Pro Standards level didn't take immediate shape. After the chairman's ousted tenure, years of lesser-qualified manikins filled the position with little more than a clerical regard. The breadth and potential power to do good things fell by the wayside.

Then union president Keith Wilkins had previously installed a national chairman who'd never served on a Pilot Professional Standards committee, not understanding its nuances nor potential. I'd served several years at the Pro Standards national level, once even shushed when I mentioned a suicide prevention protocol. Upon his vacancy, I interviewed for the national chair position to see it again given to someone else.

I sat patiently on the national committee until, one day, the dream of active human intervention awakened to a new reality.

I finally got my wish when a like-minded group of pilots converged upon DFW to create committees that support crewmembers and their families in times of duress.

Wilkins called to let me know his choice for the National Professional Standards Chairman position.

"Hey, Tom. I've decided to give the job to Doug Wood," he said briskly.

"I don't know him," I said, wondering if he'd again lowered it to a minion position.

"I guess this means you'll be leaving the committee," he concluded, sounding like I was one of ten calls he needed to make and anxious to move to the next one.

"Of course not." He'd expected me to take my marbles and play somewhere else. My hope resided in the position being filled by someone of similar vision, though I feared and concluded the contrary. I couldn't have been more wrong.

With the support of the union hierarchy empowering our vision, the committee found traction and direction. Fellow committee members Ron France, Trace Lott, Pat McGinn, Bill White, Art Hyatt, and Clark Walker shared the dream, molding it into our common vision.

The national committee's role grew exponentially to capture and interact with other committees creating a web of pilot assistance. The Allied Pilots Association set the airline industry's gold standard of pilot assistance. Numerous committees, including Project Wingman, Critical Incident Response Program, Sudden Grief Response Program, and HIMS (Human Interventional Medical Study), provided help and support to pilots and their families. Pilot Professional Standards now had viable union resources, supported by compassionate, resourceful flight offices throughout the system.

Historically, pilots prided themselves on never meeting their supervisors. The belief was, "If I meet the chief pilot, I've probably done something wrong. "Director of Flight Operations East, Captain Mark Cronin, single-handedly changed the course of that thinking.

Three words frequently attached themselves to Captain Cronin's name.

"He gets it."

Captain Cronin built a network of chief pilots who advocated for the pilot group and served the needs of pilots. Being like-minded, the Professional Standards National Committee often met with Mark and several chief pilots to develop strategies for helping the pilot group.

He wasn't beyond antics. I once saw him get into a wrestling match with a younger chief pilot and nearly kick over a buffet table. You haven't laughed until you've seen two grown men in suits wrestling like ten-year-old kids, but it was an extension of Mark's pure nature.

"What we are in this moment is what truly matters. Someday in the distant future, we will likely be sitting in an assisted living community, drooling and clapping our hands, saying, 'Yay, today is applesauce day!' When we're sitting there hooked up to a suitcase full of oxygen bottles, it is a compassionate life that we should look back at. It is moments like these that will have been those of true meaning."

Mark made no promises to the supervisors and instead committed to the pilot group's well-being. He reiterated on more than one occasion that if any chief pilot was not tending to the needs of their line pilots, to please let him know, and they would be reassigned and relegated to flying the line the next day. Not taking care of our own met zero tolerance.

"Be a steward of your profession," he'd say. The price of his advocacy was our professionalism, and most of our pilots complied.

His perspective bridged the gap between the union and management. To this day, his intention resides within the leadership of the pilot group.

Chief Pilots have become approachable and cordial problem solvers and have forged a common ground. The unions embrace their pilots' needs and advocate for their well-being. Airline management recognizes the importance of this and works hand-in-hand to create solutions.

Care and feeding required careful engagement like any relationship, but we'd planted the seeds.

14

SHANGHAI SURPRISE

FISTS OF FURY

"Let me get this straight. During the layover, the whole crew went to a local bar and got into a heated argument. It escalated out of control, resulting in you all jumping over tables, throwing chairs and beating the tar out of each other. The next day you all got on the airplane and flew it home as if nothing had ever happened. Is that correct?"

"Yes, sir," said the pilot on the other end of the call.

"Damn. You all okay, otherwise?"

"Yes, sir. Just some scratches and bruises. I'll send you a pic."

I opened the file expecting to see only mild contusions, but this guy had taken a beating. Parallel scratches marked his forehead, and a thin dark ring circled beneath a swollen eye.

"Whoa, man. You weren't kidding!"

"It really got elevated," he added. "That purser is crazy. She jumped across the table like an angry cat. Then her boyfriend jumped in."

"Who's her boyfriend?'

"The captain."

I rubbed my temples and considered my approach.

"For starters, keep a lid on this. If it goes beyond me, I can guarantee you'll all be terminated."

"Yes, sir."

What happens in Vegas stays in Vegas, except this happened in Shanghai. Sticks and stones might break your bones, but barstools and beer mugs leave a serious mark too.

After 20 years of service, I'd arguably entered the twilight of my tenure at the Pilot Professional Standards Committee. Most volunteers lasted a year or two before the badgering ate them up. During my time, I'd served on both local and national committees, having handled hundreds of calls.

The weightiness of this call mandated pushing it up to our national committee from the local level. Complex cases were always bumped up to more seasoned members of the committee. I'd dealt with plenty of cases involving heated conflict, but this one even put *me* back on my heels.

The crew returned to the layover hotel after being tossed from the bar. Some of the blows had landed, evidenced by lacerated and bruised faces. These weren't some drunk dock workers throwing hands behind a local tavern over an allegiance to a soccer team. These were professional airline crew members.

They'd compartmentalized the issue, returned to their professional personas, and safely flew the aircraft back to its destination. They'd observed standard operating procedures and had no extraneous conversation for fourteen hours.

Once they returned, they had gone home, again becoming heated as their significant others scornfully inspected their injuries. The knives came back out, and the episode reignited.

My job was to impose a resolution, and it took more than a few calming breaths for me to speak with a peaceful demeanor.

Flight crews, upon more than one occasion, have faced termination for less consequential acts. An employee needed only to make subtle physical contact with a fellow employee to face termination. In other cases, their actions during layovers brought consequences.

In one instance, a crew was guilty of nothing more than having a good time on a layover at a Caribbean destination bar. They'd become boisterous and got a little rowdy at worst. Unfortunately, one of the bar patrons turned out to be a vengeful public official. She asked about the group, and the bartender said they were an airline crew enjoying themselves. Feeling put off and perhaps overly empowered, she flexed her authority by contacting airline management. The airline panicked in a hurried, if not fearful act to appease the government official. Upon arrival in Miami, the captain of the flight crew had his employment terminated. He eventually got his job back but, to this day, endures the burden of those events.

With the agreement of all parties concerned, Professional Standards would contain events. If we lost that containment, it was anybody's game. Once again, our dialogue and protocol were far different from corporate's due to their legal requirements. As a peer-to-peer group, our latitude for how to respond was broader and more colorful. And all agreed to accept and comply with the committee's decision.

With this firmly in mind, my first words to the brawling crewmembers focused on their potential termination.

"Your jobs will be over," I said, "you'll leave your occupations with this disgraceful mark on your records."

"I don't care! I'll take this to the media. I'll sue." My words were falling on deaf ears.

Though they claimed to be seeking a resolution to the problem, I felt more like a referee. My face reddened with frustration as I tried to mediate the situation, and they raised their voices toward me.

"The media won't care. Try finding a lawyer who thinks you'll win a case where you got fired for getting into a barfight with a fellow pilot on a layover!"

I returned to my composure. At this point, a cool-off was necessary.

I said, "I'm going on a trip for the next few days. I want you all to sit with your thoughts and think about who butters your bread. If we haven't resolved this when I return, it will go to a place none of us wants it to go." In moments like this, I wondered how I could do this as volunteer work.

When we reconvened the conversation a few days later, tempers had cooled, and the waters had calmed.

Among my nonnegotiable demands was that none would ever again occupy the same airplane.

"If any of you happen to be in Flight Operations at the same time, don't even look at each other."

I felt like I was scolding children who had gotten into a fight on a playground.

All involved complied with my direction, kept their jobs, and never flew on the same airplane again.

15

A Hot One

From Quiet to Chaos

The workload of Pro Standards often escalated from quiet to chaos. My dedicated number allowed a directed confinement of that chaos.

"Hi, Ron," I answered.

"Hey Tom, we've got a hot one. Do you want it?" he replied. I could tell by the haste in his voice he had enough on his plate. We'd had a quieter-than-normal week, but calls came in bunches as a surge of activity ensued.

"Sure, what's up?"

"I've got a couple of guys going at it on a trip out of Las Vegas heading to LAX. They promised to keep it all business until LA, but the first officer said he won't go any further."

When pilots sit next to each other for days at a time, they talk. Sometimes, they talk about the wrong things. An issue could stem from something as ridiculous as a difference in political or religious views but can generate enough friction to affect the safety of the flight deck. We'd see a significant uptick in flight deck conflicts during contract negotiations or elections. This case had all the ingredients. Some guys couldn't leave their opinions at home.

"I'll call the chief in LAX and have him removed from the sequence. It's an Airbus crew base, so they should have enough time to get another flight crewmember for the next leg."

The chief pilots had been instructed not to ask why we needed someone removed but often had a good idea. A couple of strongly worded phone calls would be made in the coming days. The pilots would be counseled, and a future incident might be averted. Calling out a reserve pilot over an unnecessary conflict at the front of a multi-million-dollar airplane always warranted a follow-up, complete with a tongue-lashing and some solid perspective.

The chief pilot made his necessary entries to remove the pilot from the balance of the flight sequence. Crew Tracking became involved to ensure the flight schedule stayed on track. One pilot missing a flight could have a rippling effect on subsequent flights and potentially affect hundreds of passengers with downline connections. Crew Schedule consulted a short callout list, and the schedule maintained continuity.

Within fifteen minutes, the appropriate calls had been made. Somewhere in the LA basin, a replacement first officer donned their uniform and headed to the airport.

When this happened for legitimate reasons such as illness or family emergencies, the system's intention and use resembled a well-oiled machine. Incorporating these elements to appease two pilots who differed in political opinion struck a nerve.

I sat and contemplated the tasks I'd completed. These types of interactions chiseled away at me. "I'm getting too old for this shit," I said aloud, wondering how much more bickering I could handle.

The phone rang again, this time with a different caller. When it rains, it pours, I thought. Probably someone calling to complain about the temperature of their crew meal. I took a deep breath, dismissing the annoyance of the previous event.

"Pilot Professional Standards, Tom speaking."

"Hey Tom, I need some guidance." I detected an edge unlike what I usually heard. The voice trembled with angst.

"Sure, tell me what's going on, and I'll do my best to help."

"I was just charged with a felony. I believe I have a drinking problem, and I'm scheduled to fly a trip next week."

I took a deep breath.

"Well. I can agree with the first of those two statements, but the third one is incorrect. We're going to have you pulled from your flying status and get you the help you need."

A week earlier, Carl Metz stood alongside his colleagues at the International Flight Operations area of Chicago O'Hare Airport. He wore a crisp shirt and pressed uniform, portraying a clean-cut crewmember. He scoured the details of the Paris-bound flight plan displayed on his company iPad.

Carl had come to work sober, concealing a secret. He put on his best face and shared an amiable smile while hiding in plain sight. I said hello and returned to my work, unaware that this fellow pilot masked a fierce struggle with addictions to alcohol and gambling.

The bright green lanyard imprinted with the words "Professional Standards" draped around my neck served not only to identify me as a committee member but also as an invitation.

Carl tilted in my direction and nearly uttered, "May I speak to you for a moment?" but lost his nerve and decided to hold his tongue. A misdirected code of pride reeled him back, assuring him he could slay the daunting beast within.

He flew his trip, kept to himself, and returned to a home once filled with vibrance but now void of the love that once greeted him at the threshold.

A son and a daughter once cheered, "Daddy, daddy!" while encircling him with hugs.

Instead, the vacant darkness of a recent divorce met him at the door.

After leaning hard into a bottle of Jack Daniels whiskey, the pain of emptiness and isolation diverted him from much-needed rest. He ignored the burdens of fatigue and intoxication and drove to a local casino.

Once seated at a blackjack table, Carl's scant focus betrayed his acuity and caused him to drain his wallet of the week's earnings.

"What's with all the crap cards?!" he yelled.

The dealer raised an eye at the pit boss, who'd already tuned in.

Something internally began to snap as he watched the dealer slide his lost money through the drop box slot.

"Can you deal me one damn decent hand?!"

Unfiltered rage overtook Carl's demeanor as he berated the dealer in an elevated display of exasperation.

Heavy-handed security guards dragged Carl away from the table and escorted him to the couch of a private room, where he fell asleep. He woke soon after and pushed away well-intending employees, escaped through the casino doors, and stumbled into the driver's seat of his car. Tires squealed as a security officer leaped out of the way of the vehicle, barely escaping with his life. As the car bolted from the lot, the casino alerted authorities to avert an even more tragic outcome.

Only a few miles down the road, a State Police cruiser caught up to Carl. He pulled to the side of the highway and was taken into custody.

That night, he sat in a dank cinder block holding cell, feeling the firm thud of hitting rock bottom. Thoughts of the charges – Driving Under the Influence and Attempted Manslaughter swirled with a new word: suicide.

The time had come to confront the beast, and Carl knew he couldn't fight this battle alone.

The union and airline had united to build a system to help pilots in need. Once nothing more than an idea, it now held the strength and fortitude of a formidable entity. The two factions had put all differences aside to unite in the common ideal of protecting and serving the needs of the pilot group. They backed their intentions with both human and financial commitment.

The following morning, the collective efforts of many joined to help Carl start the road to recovery.

Carl's battle would begin with a single step in the right direction. His addiction would attempt to tighten its grip when he took that step, punishing him with the pain of withdrawal. It would pull at his mind and body, promising refuge for just a sip.

He'd bargained away enough of his life. The exchange had left his home and his body broken. From rock bottom he'd pulled himself up by his bootstraps, made a call, and gained the support of a dedicated and compassionate team.

He knew what he had at stake and would prevail.

The airline and union saw alcoholism as a treatable and curable disease. It required a team to help Carl and others with his plight. But the outcome of his battle and those who shared it could save a life, a job, and often the families and friends surrounding them.

Carl invoked the discipline of his previous military training to take on and defeat alcoholism.

I checked on him often, hoping for positive progress. He'd plead his felony to a lessor charge.

Carl re-engaged with his children, again the sober pillar of strength he'd once been to them. His home, now clear of the remnants of his past, became inviting to the company of others as he replaced his addictions with culinary skills.

Many months later he had his day in court.

"It appears you've battled some demons," said the somber judge. "More importantly, it appears you've defeated those demons."

"Yes, your honor. I have."

"I've taken note of your military service and compliment you on your successful rehabilitation." The judge sentenced Carl to fines and community service.

A year later, Carl re-engaged his mastery with aircraft and successfully completed requalification training at the airline. He returned to work, a new man, and an inspiration to others.

Note: Carl's recovery mirrors that of many others, diligently meeting the criteria of the HIMS program. Now sober for years, Carl is one of hundreds of examples of the high percentage of pilots who have successfully redeemed themselves, reassembled their lives, and returned to flying.

16

Captain, Be the Captain.

Plays Well with Others

Several months before my final flight, I had a reprehensible woman removed from the airplane.

She struck me as someone who sprayed nastiness at anyone in her proximity. Passengers can be irritable, I get that, but nothing about this flight itself could have driven her level of annoyance.

The flight deck happy meter was pegged far right. We had a great crew, no maintenance items, correct catering, and literal clear skies ahead. A promising push of tailwinds to Barcelona strengthened the vibe. When things flow seamlessly, blissful energy flows over the crew like cherry wine.

We'd completed our initial flight deck safety checks, and I stepped out of the captain's seat to chat with the purser. Marz, an astute and patient flight attendant and longtime friend, met me in the forward galley for a quick briefing.

"7 hours, 52 minutes, no cabin items in the logbook, a slight possibility of a bump or two about three hours into the flight," I briefed.

I showed Marz the weather pattern on my iPad and pointed at a depiction of a small area of turbulence, lending my ear to a slight elevation in the business class cabin.

A woman demanded that the flight attendant stow her bag in the overhead compartment. I peeked down the aisle to appraise the situation. The flight attendant imparted a firm but courteous response and politely stepped away. The passenger's apparel and bling indicated wealth as she plopped into her premium-class seat like royalty. I have no issue with this, but our flight attendants aren't servants or bag porters.

I pivoted toward Marz.

"What's the ruckus?" I asked.

"We've got a spicy one in 3C. She already unloaded some anger on me," she answered. She gave me a look that reflected many years of dealing with this type of passenger.

"Let me know if she elevates," I replied, suspecting my hopes might be dashed.

The decision to remove a passenger should never be made as one of vengeance but rather of consequence. This person and her husband had purchased an expensive ticket intending to enjoy a European vacation. I hoped that would be the case and returned to the flight deck.

Up front, we completed our before-start checklist; I made a quick welcome aboard PA and looked out to see the final bag light illuminated on the gate display. Cargo doors latched closed, and only an open forward passenger door entry symbol remained on the flight deck synoptic display. *Maybe some last-minute passengers,* I thought.

In the mid-galley, exasperated cabin crewmembers huddled for a pow-wow, searching for a solution.

"Okay, who wants to deal with her?" one chimed.

"I think her connecting flight inbound was on a broom," said another.

"No kidding, she's as mean as a rattlesnake."

Without another word, the eyes of the group shifted to Guillermo. Guillermo, a walking sedative blessed with the calmest and kindest of dispositions, nodded in agreement, aware of the task he'd been drafted into. He broke from the huddle to engage the salty woman.

He walked up the aisle and faced her squarely, imparting a courteous smile.

"Madam, may I bring you anything to drink?" he inquired.

His gracious approach met immediate condescension.

She snorted. "If you want to talk to me, you'd better learn to speak better English, you *@%!," she said along with a racial slur.

Marz relayed the news a moment later, standing in the flight deck doorway.

"We're not doing this. Have her escorted off the airplane." I responded.

A slight lift at the corner of Marz's mouth suggested she agreed with my decision as she turned toward the cabin and disappeared.

Even on the best days, air travel involves stress. A lot of that happens before even getting to the airplane. Driving to Chicago O'Hare Airport can present notoriously unpredictable traffic. Passengers then deal with long check-in and security lines inside the jam-packed terminal of one of the busiest airports on Earth.

Sensory overload proves overwhelming and tests the patience of the most stoic veteran air travelers.

"The captain has to be the captain, and you can't abuse the crew. I don't like bullies," I said. "I don't think anyone has slapped down the reverse Uno card on that woman for a while."

I looked at the other two pilots, who nodded, knowing she'd stepped over the line. I had no choice but to insist that she find an alternative means of transportation.

Passengers applauded as the shamefaced woman and her husband exited onto the jet bridge. As the woman's husband stood up, he threw his champagne glass across the seat, portraying a final, inclusive act of rebellion. She probably beat him with the heel of her shoe on the way home anyway.

Despite the cheers, seeing this scornful person and her husband face the public humiliation of being marched off the airplane bothered me.

The dynamics of engagement come into play when dealing with fallible humans, and they're essential when playing a leadership role. We can handle a cloud on a sunny day, but it's time to change course when that cloud becomes a thunderstorm.

Minutes later, we pushed back from the gate with a blissful crew and two empty business-class seats. The flight progressed as effortlessly as predicted, landing in the small hours of the morning in Barcelona.

That evening, beneath a pastel Spanish sky, rooftop, and poolside, the crew met to informally debrief.

Guillermo walked over and handed me a beverage.

"Captain, I want to thank you for standing up for me and the crew."

"Of course," I said. "And thank you, but that's my job. You didn't need to buy me a drink."

The airline, regarded for its consistent intolerance of racism, stood behind us and my decision to remove the passenger one hundred percent.

17

ON CALL

DRINKING THE TEA

"This Cabernet is *outstanding*. Are you sure you don't want some, Tom?"

Matt Wolfe couldn't tell wine from Windex, and I wasn't taking the bait anyway. He eyed his tilted glass and swirled the contents in a mock connoisseur fashion.

"I'd love to have some, but I'm on call."

I sipped my iced tea, set it back on the table, and pushed the lemon down into the glass with the tip of my straw.

"They haven't needed you for weeks," he prodded. "What's the chance of them calling? Haven't most of the international flights gone out already this evening?"

"Maybe, but a couple are still at the gate, and the others occasionally turn around and need to be recrewed."

"The second he takes a sip of that wine, the phone will ring," offered Des.

"Guaranteed! Besides, they pay me to be ready to go when I'm on short call. I learned that the hard way one afternoon on the 12th fairway at the Kalamazoo Country Club. A rainstorm blew through, and I got soaked – I looked like a cat that fell into a swimming pool. I was far from dry clothes, my car, and the airport. Bam - Crew Schedule calls me for a trip right then. It was almost like they knew."

"After that, I promised myself I'd always be showered and ready - a tank full of gas, an overnight bag in the trunk, and my uniform hanging behind the driver's seat. Doesn't stop me from enjoying this *outstanding* glass of iced tea, though," I teased as I picked up my glass and swirled the contents.

"Sounds like you miss out on a lot of fun."

"On the contrary. If anything, it's better for me. I make sure I get adequate sleep and find myself at the gym more."

Matt contemplated the idea as he downed the rest of his Cab.

We said our goodbyes and headed home.

So far, all remained quiet on the home front, with the tentative plan of an uneventful evening. Des yawned and trotted upstairs to get ready for bed. As she disappeared around the railing, my phone lit up with the image of an airplane, and a familiar ringtone played. Crew Schedule summons.

With thousands of daily flights and over 16,000 pilots to fly them, broken sequences requiring crew reassignments are inevitable. Whether triggered by maintenance, weather, legality, or a pilot who misread their schedule, Crew Schedule runs a 24/7/365 operation, to keep aircraft manned.

"Hello, Captain Huitema; it's Patti in Crew Schedule. We need you for a trip this evening…." The litany had to be exact, including sign-in time. It's a recorded line, and they've had to review a call along the way when things run amiss.

"Thanks, Patti; I'll get there as soon as possible," I confirmed for the recording. I'd known Patti Armstrong since the 80s, and now that we had the formality out of the way, I could ask her if she had any intel on how the trip came open.

"Last minute sick call?"

"Nah," she answered. "The captain called in fatigued. Apparently, he had a rough day at the layover hotel and couldn't pre-load his sleep. A bunch of angry employees got boisterous and put on a loud protest. We'll probably have to pull out of that place until things settle."

A noisy hotel can cost an airline significant revenue if it takes a flight crew out of the game. The protest left the pilot too fatigued to fly the long leg to a European destination. He observed the fatigue policy and notified the company that he didn't feel safe having 300 lives in his hands. A smart move. Fatigue is dangerous and self-assessing a "fit for duty" condition is essential. They pulled him from the assignment, but now the captain's seat on the London flight needed to be filled, and I was the next person on the reserve list to go.

I hung up and yelled up the stairs.

"Hey, Des."

"Yeah?"

"I gotta roll - just got called for a London trip."

"Ah, London. Sounds like fun. Want some company?"

"Heck yeah."

"Okay."

She spoke as if I'd asked if she wanted me to bring her a glass of water. Pilot spouses live unique lives and learn to expect the unexpected. She usually packed a bag for such an occasion in case date night transformed into date night deluxe.

Within minutes, we pulled onto Interstate 94 toward Chicago O'Hare. Des drove while I squeezed into my uniform and pulled up the flight plan on my company iPad.

A light traffic flow helped us get to the airport without delay. After parking and hurrying through security, I saw the supervisory agent, Raj, standing and staring down from the end of the concourse adjacent to our departure gate. He's a six-foot-five-inch statue you can pick out at quite a distance.

He recognized Des and me as we walked together down the concourse, me in uniform and Des a tattooed hippy farm girl wearing jeans.

He greeted us with his warm, familiar smile, handed Des a boarding pass, and said, "I got you a good seat."

Raj, a man of impeccable character and a corporate pilot on his days off, was the glue to our Chicago international gate operation. Every airline could use an asset like him; luckily, he worked for us.

I hustled down the jet bridge onto the airplane and turned left. Upon entering the flight deck, I said," Hey guys, how's it going?

"Good Cap. Everything is plugged in, and we're ready to roll," answered the first officer. They'd preflighted and programmed everything, and the aircraft sat ready. I love it when a plan comes together.

I settled into the familiar nest, got organized, ran the appropriate checklists, briefed, and soon after, our Boeing 787-9 Dreamliner pushed back from the gate.

About 20 rows back, Des had plopped into her "good" seat.

A passenger leaned toward her and jokingly said, "Are you running a bit late this evening?"

Des grinned, "Yeah, but I brought your captain with me."

A few hours after leveling at our cruise altitude, the lights of civilization below us became sparse. The darkness of barren land now separated distant specks of light blending to an unseen horizon. The vast expanse of Newfoundland unfolded beneath the nose as we traversed high above its untamed wilderness at over 500 mph. Passengers dined on freshly cooked cuisine, lounged while watching the latest movies on their monitors, and surfed satellite internet.

The pedestal printer buzzed and spat out our North Atlantic Track clearance; tonight's aerial highway comprised of track coordinates. Oceanic entry points separated aircraft like rolling toll gates; each assigned a specific speed and altitude to its European exit gate. Less than one hundred years earlier, a single-engine airplane piloted by Charles Lindberg had traversed these skies in the first solo trans-Atlantic crossing.

Our relief pilot, Craig, returned to the flight deck holding a cup of coffee. Each pilot would get about a two-hour break. The first break was taken by the relief pilot, who tried to rest in the crew bunk to the tune of galley carts and dishes clanging below.

"Get some sleep, buddy?" Craig and I had become friends outside of work.

"A little bit," he said as he cleared the last remnants of sleep inertia.

"We're on time, up 300 on fuel. Gander looks like our best diversion alternate for medical or maintenance." I continued the key points of the briefing and then stepped to the back to say hello to Des before hitting the rack.

"You wanna meet the captain?" Des raised her eyes toward me, unimpressed.

"Sure."

"This is why I drink iced tea at dinner."

"Yeah, right?"

A few minutes later, I squeezed into the bunk, drew the curtain, and closed my eyes. The memory of sleeping in the tiny baggage compartment of a single-engine Cessna parked on the ramp of the Grand Canyon Airport entered my mind. I'd come a long way.

PART TWO - DYING

18

FINAL FLIGHT

BARREL ROLL

We sliced through the night sky at 41,000 feet, sitting on top of the world in an empty Dreamliner. Air whispered over the composite nose and curved windshields, allowing for quiet flight deck conversation.

"I wonder if this thing could do a barrel roll?"

My first officer, Nick, sported a mischievous grin. He faced forward, but his eyes moved in my direction, searching for a reaction rather than a response.

"Pretty twisted thought, Nick," I teased.

Empty airplanes make for odd contemplations. Many pilots think about this, and a few have acted on those contemplations, though never with the Dreamliner.

Our Chicago to Dallas/Fort Worth flight flew without passengers, flight attendants, or cargo. Some pilots dread maintenance repositioning ferry flights, but I enjoyed feeling the airplane's lightweight performance. Having demonstrated full operational knowledge of the forward galley espresso maker, I proudly held a resulting doppio cappuccino while infatuated with an unfiltered view of the stars above.

During a trans-Atlantic crossing, an electrical malfunction had hobbled the airplane we were ferrying. It had diverted to Reykjavik, Iceland, and a second aircraft retrieved the temporarily stranded passengers. Airline maintenance techs flew to repair the plane in Iceland, and another crew brought the partially patched-up airplane back to Chicago. A subsequent inspection revealed the need for more in-depth mechanical repairs before its return to international service, thus our repositioning to the more substantially equipped DFW maintenance facility.

Aside from a humorous and imaginative co-pilot, nothing was notable about this flight.

When it came to Nick's barrel roll question, more than one pilot had demonstrated the answer. Yes, an airliner can do a barrel roll. The most famous was when the chief of flight testing, "Tex" Johnson, rolled the prototype Boeing 707 over Lake Washington in 1955. Astounded boaters below looked up to see a jaw-dropping view of an upside-down airliner. Tex thought it was so fun he did it twice.

A story exists from decades ago of one of our aircraft being barrel rolled during a ferry flight. Unlike today, aircraft of the time lacked specific and transmittable monitoring of all flight parameters. After the pilots landed and taxied to the maintenance hangers, they thought they'd gotten away with it. They very well may have, but blue water from the toilets had splashed onto the walls and ceiling of each lavatory, revealing that the airplane had been inverted. When mechanics inspected the aircraft, they noticed and reported the mess. A quick interrogation of the flight data recorders unveiled the truth.

Busted.

The pilots who flew this airplane did carpet time in the chief pilot's office, had some serious explaining to do, and may have been out looking for another job.

Historically, large jet aircraft have been asked to do many things that fall well outside the norm, usually as an unintended result of non-standard operating procedures. They've been flipped and sub-sonic wings have exceeded the speed of sound. But despite having been accidentally forced far outside their certified realm, the aircraft have typically survived these obscure events. In comparison, a simple barrel roll marginally pushes those aerodynamic boundaries.

I returned my attention from the oversized flight deck windows to my first officer. Feigning curious disapproval, I answered Nick.

"The short answer is yes, not that it would ever happen."

"After about 35 degrees of bank, the airplane's Flight Control Computers would start to fight back and attempt to decrease the bank to re-level the wings. The maneuver would feel awkward, not that I'd have the least desire to confirm such knowledge. I'm a straight-and-level kind of guy."

Nick considered the information.

"So, bad idea then?" he smirked.

"Really bad, Nick. The 787 also transmits 2000 pieces of information twice per second. You'd make headlines before the maneuver even finished," I added. "Now that you've got that thought out of your mind let's check which direction they're landing at DFW."

Our thoughts shifted back to the business at hand.

We pulled up and reviewed the airport arrival information, cross-checking and confirming the arrival points in the Flight Management Computer.

A few minutes later, air traffic control issued a clearance. "American 9055, descend at pilot's discretion to maintain flight level 230." We answered, yielding our seat atop the troposphere. With reluctance, the aircraft's vertical navigation system delayed descent until the last moment, allowing the engines to sip fuel at cruise altitude.

Once established in the descent, our Dreamliner turned and glided effortlessly through the plotted and programmed arrival procedure, slowing, leveling, and descending to comply with speed and crossing restrictions.

I clicked off the autopilot, loving the feeling of this beautiful flying machine in my hands while maintaining my flight proficiency. We configured and stabilized on final approach as the airplane pointed to the long parallel rows of lights that outlined Runway 17L at Dallas-Ft. Worth Airport.

Once above the runway threshold, I pulled the thrust levers back to flight idle, and the aircraft's eight main landing gear tires reached down to find the pavement. The flexed composite wings settled, letting go of their last grasp of the air. As we decelerated, my left hand released the control yoke for the last time and reached for the steering tiller.

With no aircraft on the approach behind us, we could use the long runway for a high-speed taxi and allow her to roll to the distant turn-off leading to the maintenance ramp. A mechanic holding lighted wands stood waiting and marshaled us onto our parking spot beside a mobile airstair. A truck with the word

"Maintenance" stenciled across the door sat in front of a massive hangar.

Without passengers or flight attendants to bid farewell, I toted my bags down the airstair and, as always, glanced back to take in the beautiful airplane I loved.

We gladly accepted a ride to the hotel from the mechanic who'd helped us park the airplane. Like me, he'd been a part of the airline industry since the mid-nineteen eighties, and a glory days conversation ensued.

Little did I know I had just flown the final flight of my airline career.

19

FIT TO DIE

YOU ONLY LIVE TWICE

Six weeks before the world stopped, I'd celebrated my 60th birthday.

That day, I took a longer-than-usual inventory of the guy staring back in the mirror, concluding he hadn't aged too badly. My razor hadn't moved from its spot on the counter in three days, evidenced by the salt and pepper blend around my chin. A few silver strands had begun to sprout near my temples. The crow's feet around my eyes deepened with a smile.

"I guess I've got some miles left," I concluded.

My yearly birthday ceremony brought me to the gym for a solid workout. A lifelong commitment to exercise accounted for a healthy level of strength and energy. The trip to the gym served as an annual celebration and a recommitment to the tenets of fitness that I'd followed since my mid-teens. It affirmed my quest for health and longevity.

I walked into the Kalamazoo Powerhouse Gym and scanned in my membership fob. The attendant looked up and said, "Happy birthday!" alerted by the display on her computer check-in screen.

"Thanks, the big six zero," I boasted. I never made much of a deal about my birthday, but this number was a milestone and made me officially entitled to a host of senior discounts. More so, I wanted the world to see the defiant strength available at this age rather than the decrepitation often associated with the advancement of years.

My friend Steve Hutson put down his dumbbells, looked over, and met my eye. "Happy Birthday, old man," he jabbed. In a place where the faces I'd seen for years looked the other way; he always shot a welcoming smile.

"Thanks, dude."

"Now get to work. Those weights aren't going to lift themselves."

"Yeah, right? It's only gravity. Maybe I'll go a little heavier today."

I loved the carnal appeal of lifting things and enjoyed heaving anything other than sleeper couches.

As I pressed a stack of weights, I could hear Steve from across the gym. "Push hard, brother! One more rep! You got this!" Every gym could use a guy like him. Half the fun of his workout entailed motivating others with his affable manner. Despite his size, strength, and fitness level, his greater focus always pointed to the people around him. Reverence carried the greatest weight.

I finished the set and shot him a thumbs up. Though we only occasionally saw each other outside the gym, we knew each other well. Many years of sentences between sets totaled a solid friendship.

I took a couple of selfies with my buddies, planning a fitness advocacy social media post. The connective nature of our passion blended with the sweat as years passed.

At the end of the workout, I decided to take it down to the floor. I could hold a "burner" of a forearm plank for three minutes, but I'd worked and challenged my way past this number over the last several months.

Daft Punk's "Aerodynamic" remix would serve me well with its 6:07 run time; I needed only to listen to the music. The clock is a distraction, and looking at it made time creep. Earbuds in, volume up, let's do this. With my favorite song playing, I closed my eyes and focused inward on the strength of my core.

My body shook slightly toward the song's end, with only a mild objection from my shoulders. The tune played its final notes, and I stayed locked in position for a few more seconds. As I looked down and tapped the screen on my iPhone, the stopwatch function lit up to display 6 minutes and 36 seconds.

"Oh yeah, immortal me!" I said. I'd defeated aging for another year.

We consider our health and fitness routines to be a method of preserving ourselves while creating longevity. A healthy lifestyle makes assurances but no guarantees. We are, unfortunately, only as strong as our weakest necessary component. The weakest link in my chain would soon announce itself. Mine had first made itself known in my teens.

"You've got a click in your heart," said the doctor, the end of his chilly stethoscope sliding around on my chest.

"What does that mean?"

"It's common. Nothing to worry about."

Each click allowed blood to backflow into the left atrium of my heart. Over decades, the blood flow reversing past partially closing valve leaflets became more prevalent. The pressure severely enlarged the left atrial chamber. Other chambers of the heart also grew to the point of becoming severely oversized. Semi-annual physical exams and annual EKGs failed to disclose any issues.

The malfunction was a ticking time bomb. It wasn't a matter of if my heart was going to stop. It was a matter of when.

20

Death Grip

A Rough Night

The final grains fell from a 15-minute sand timer neatly mounted to the inside sauna wall.

"That's enough for me," Des sighed, sporting a rosy glaze.

"I think I'll cook for another 15 minutes before I come up."

I reached over and flipped the hourglass.

"Not too much, okay?" she said, recognizing my propensity to push too hard.

"Fair enough," I assured her.

Des exited the sauna and trekked up the stairs to the bedroom.

The new sauna provided a connective and meditative experience. It offered a peaceful place to calm the mental waters and embraced us in a blanket of warmth before bed.

Recapturing an unfinished portion of the basement had served as a victory. The catchall for the remnants of each child's youth culminated in a hoarder's paradise. On rainy days, I'd sift through the mess, donating or disposing of unneeded items to clear the space, eventually rewarded with a reclaimed area. Neatly stacked matching plastic totes, now hidden from view, sat upon utility shelves in a separate area.

In the newly christened spa room, a cozy rug spanned the floor beneath soft Tuscan sunset mood lighting. Adorned with terry cloth robes and fluffy white rolled-up towels, wooden tongue and groove panels completed the blissful ambiance.

Desiree's words about not pushing too hard hung in the lavender-scented air. I paid them a moment of thought and ladled more water over the sizzling lava rocks, wondering why so many things in my life amounted to a contest against myself. I'd beaten personal bests in foot races but paid with aching knees. I lifted more weight than ever to be rewarded with torn muscles.

The Nietzsche quote, "What doesn't kill you makes you stronger," chanted through the heat.

Fun fact. A 160-degree, 20-minute sauna four times a week reduces your chances of a cardiac event by 51%.

My usual routine allowed the heat to penetrate for fifteen or twenty minutes. More pliant muscles cooperated in ceremonial stretching. Usually, a warm shower followed, and the lull of sleep beckoned.

On this night, my thoughts turned.

The latest rave boasted of the health benefits of cold plunges. The Finnish set their saunas to broil and, after some time, would jump in the snow. Celebrities climbed aboard to advocate hot-to-cold transition, declaring the benefits to their followers, naming anatomical responses and chemicals that fell well outside my finite vocabulary. The number of cardiologists who advise the contrary has since stacked up, but celebrity endorsements get more clicks.

I decided to test the experience by employing a fast temperature transition. Fire and ice had such a trendy sound, and what did I have to lose?

The hourglass again expired. I'd clocked 30 minutes in the hotbox. The thermometer read 170 degrees Fahrenheit. I stumbled out and noticed the customary blanket of comfort and tranquility hadn't presented itself.

"Let's do this," I whispered, ignoring the heat exhaustion.

Without allowing transition time, I started phase two of the hot-to-cold experience. I scurried into the adjacent bathroom and stepped under the frigid waterfall of a drenching showerhead. This amounted to nearly 130 degrees of immediate temperature change. I held a gasp as the frigid water soaked my chest and head.

Nausea overcame me as the water poured. My breath became choppy and a grip of dizziness and discomfort took hold and deepened.

"Oh no, this isn't good," I muttered.

I needed to get near someone in case I fainted. I smacked the water shutoff, wrapped a towel around myself, wobbled up the stairs to the bedroom, and flopped onto the mattress next to Des.

I'd be alive for another forty-five seconds.

Desiree, who was nearly always sound asleep when I crawled into bed, sat awake reading. We're often not in the same house at the same time. Our travel schedules put us in various places, and even when we're home, the challenges of circadian rhythms commonly put us in different rooms so that the other can sleep.

"Would you like me to turn off the light?" she queried.

"No, give me a second," I said in the calmest voice I could muster.

I didn't want to alarm her with what I hoped would be a passing sensation, but I didn't want the room to be dark if it worsened.

I gasped and sputtered for air as my fists clenched in front of me and my eyes rolled back.

Ventricular fibrillation. Cardiac arrest.

The lower chambers of my heart quivered and twitched, no longer delivering blood by expanding and squeezing. Without immediate intervention, death was only a few minutes away.

Desiree shook me as I convulsed and began to turn blue, wondering if I'd had a seizure. She called 911.

"He's unresponsive! Unresponsive! Send someone!" she screamed and began administering life-saving CPR.

My son, Christian, who hadn't been home from college for nearly two months, rounded the street corner in his car and arrived within 4 minutes. He walked into the house and heard Des scream for him. Also certified in CPR, he jumped in and took over compressions as they waited for EMS services to arrive with defibrillating equipment.

Christian continued compressions despite the non-responsive state of his father's lifeless body beneath him. He looked down to see slits of eyes diverge outward as I frothed at the mouth. The task demanded that he detach from emotion. He stepped outside of himself, maintaining unwavering composure. He administered mouth-to-mouth resuscitation and then re-engaged compressions on my chest.

Ten minutes after my collapse, a Portage EMS vehicle pulled in front of the house, the first of numerous emergency vehicles.

Veteran medic/firefighter Captain Clay Hollister rushed to the door toting defibrillating equipment.

He crossed the threshold and asked, "Is it Tom?"

Clay, a rugged guy with a gentle heart, also worked as a yoga teacher. He'd done a Vinyasa practice next to me two days earlier and would tell me later that being called to the scene of a friend or relative ranks among a medic's worst nightmares.

Once in the bedroom, they dropped my body to the floor. Moving me off the mattress provided a rigid surface and greater leverage to continue CPR compressions. With the defibrillator pads placed on my chest, the device searched for a shockable rhythm. Now, beyond ten minutes from my initial sudden cardiac arrest, I battled a less than two percent chance of my heart regaining a beat.

"Clear!"

Shock one.

My body lurched as the AED delivered a powerful electrical blast.

Nothing. My lifeless body fell back to the floor.

CPR continued as the AED found enough electrical activity in my heart to fire again.

"Clear!"

Shock two.

My body leaped again as if being pushed from behind.

No heartbeat.

More CPR. My chest was being pounded.

Shock three.

Nothing.

No heartbeat.

Flatline.

No longer shockable.

Dead.

The defibrillator now sat idle, unable to find necessary activity within the heart walls to trigger another shock.

Most prefer a quick death rather than the prolonged suffering of illness. I'd felt nothing more than a sharp pain and the pull of a gasp. Life had left my body, and my ending had been merciful.

At this moment, I was a corpse. I'd reached the end of the dash between my date of birth and date of death. A healthy life interrupted by a heart seizure.

Christian hugged Desiree, who stood in the hallway in shock. In death, we are no more than a memory to the living—a strong one at first. But the memory will slowly fade and give way to the healing power of time. Only God can extend the end of the dash, whether an hour, a day, or a decade.

What miracle could bring me back? Had any of a dozen occurrences not lined up in perfect order before and after this moment, this would have been the last day of my life.

"We're losing him."

"Continue the compressions."

Here another story begins, as miracles do happen.

Pride Care Ambulance Service arrived, followed by a mobile doctor. With him present, additional resources were available.

More CPR and the administration of a shot of adrenaline. With the shot, a slight activity is present in the walls of my heart. The slightest remnant of a twitch of life had re-entered my body and prompted the AED to activate.

Shock four.

My body lurched again. Still no pulse. Without a response, I'd soon have a sheet pulled over my head.

The defibrillator metronome continued to click.

Des, now sitting in the living room, looked toward the sound from upstairs. This was taking too long. Too much time had passed. He's probably gone.

An officer relayed an update.

"The doctor is here, and he'll let you know what's going on and if they plan to transport him to the hospital." Translation. He may not survive.

Shock five.

Clear.

I reanimated for a moment. During those few seconds, I fought the medics before collapsing again.

Shock six.

I reanimated momentarily, fighting like hell and swinging wildly as the medic dodged my hands.

My friend Tom Postula had been close by and stood in the room as I flailed about.

He yelled, "Tom, stop fighting them! They're trying to help you!"

My heart again stopped and I fell into silence.

CPR continued.

Shock seven, reanimated –

Medics continued holding me down as I pulled at an intubation tube. This time, the heartbeat held.

A weary Captain Clay Hollister walked out of the bedroom and conveyed the news from the top of the stairway to all waiting in the living room.

"He has a pulse."

Back to the living. Not today, Mr. Reaper. Move it along…

Twenty minutes had passed from when my heart stopped to the welcome announcement of a heartbeat.

I fought everyone around me as they placed me onto a gurney for transport to the hospital. It took six guys to secure my arms. This was a good sign.

Medics and police filled the house. Some officers had recognized the address when the initial call came over the radio. Having volunteered for nearly ten years for the Portage Police Department's Reserve Officer Division, many of those who had come to assist were old friends.

I was back among the living and stable as the Pride Care ambulance quietly brought me to Bronson Methodist Hospital.

In the Intensive Care Unit, Des and my son Christian hovered near my unconscious body.

Christian pointed the bottom of his cell phone toward me as it played Daft Punk's "Aerodynamic" remix.

"Can he hear it?" he asked.

"I don't know, but that's his song. It's the one he plays when he pushes himself."

They looked for a flutter of recognition, the raise of a brow, a twitch, anything. I lay motionless and pale, a trach tube hanging from my mouth. My heart had overcome a massive disadvantage and restarted. The next hurdle presented an even more significant challenge. Had the extended time in cardiac arrest suffocated my brain, and would the man who awakened from this nightmare be a shadow of his former self?

21

AFTERLIFE

GOING PLACES

When the curtain closed on my human life, my spirit sprang away from its anatomical clutches with purpose and direction. I propelled laterally away from my body. The assumption is that we go up but I'm here to tell you it's straight ahead. Go figure. A rectangular area of light appeared in front of me. The unmistakable form of my father awaited, flanked on either side by two distinctly human-shaped contrasts of light. The three presented together, carrying a devoutness between them. I immediately knew that each of the shapes was someone I deeply loved.

My father presented in the posture he'd carried when in his thirties. He shifted to the left, inviting me to join and engage the spirit forms. I advanced toward them as they encompassed me with love. My adoration poured into the spirits, holding an identical signature to what I felt for my children.

The words I heard next were profoundly joyous and connective.

"Hi, Daddy!"

I'd reunited with my two deceased children, Hope and Faith.

The details of their passing have been omitted to respect privacy.

In the afterlife, my father and children welcomed me as an intimate part of my heavenly family. Others awaited, but the first step in this reunion was to acquaint me with my immediate family and heal the wound of Hope and Faith's premature passing.

I'd been gifted a glimpse, and this stage showed me a fraction of an infinitely larger field.

Regarding the hereafter, it never felt so right to be wrong. I'd been given the perspective of an infinite timeline.

Agnostics question. I can't blame them. They can neither confirm nor deny yet are open to proof by objectively incorporating the tools that define tangible entities. Physics, mathematics, and the five senses quantify or negate the existence of nearly all things, including what's beyond the here and now. The issue resides in assessing what falls beyond the human senses. It's measuring the immeasurable.

How does a person blind from birth quantify sight? If everyone were blind, would the sense of vision exist?

How does a person who hasn't met God quantify His existence when the burden of proof using known factors makes dismissal much easier?

It is the power of faith. Strength in faith introduces a reassurance that empowers some yet frightens others. Faith isn't scientifically quantifiable. It is limitless to those who have it but frustrating to those who need to fit it into the framework of sensory or mathematical logic.

The human body is limited by its sensory parameters. With only those colors on the palette, you can't paint much. More exist, residing in an underdeveloped state within us. How often have we thought of someone we haven't seen in a long time, only to see or hear from them minutes later? This is scientifically unexplainable. The issue with science is that you can't only apply it where it fits and cite coincidence when lacking a quantifiable answer.

In our life beyond, senses exist too powerful to be felt within the confines of our anatomy. They become available once free of our bodily encasement.

Consider the magnification of our ability to identify and quantify love.

If love in this world is air - in the afterlife, it is a viscous liquid. It is unfiltered and unrestricted. It is pure and undiluted. It is the most magnificently clarifying and defining commodity imaginable. What I experienced could not be felt by a human body. More accurately, it required me to be free of my body to encompass its full magnitude.

My spirit form embraced an endless reality.

As I beheld the presence of my father and children, I moved in a lateral direction and basked in the utter purity of this place. A unique energy unveiled ahead and to the right, appearing somewhat like a heat signature. Its grandeur was equally powerful but different from the love I had felt between my children or father.

A ribbon of light extended in the form of a strand from the higher position above and left to the area where I now basked.

An omnipotent Presence presided from that point to my left, having arranged the reunion and allowed me to relish the moment. The power, peace, and magnificence of this Presence extended beyond what I can begin to describe in words.

God spoke.

"What you are feeling are all the kindnesses you have put into the world."

The patience of eternity resided in this realm. I sensed a pause, not in time but rather an allowance for absorbing this information.

"I want you to go back and continue your work."

A part of me wanted to stay—the relevance of earthly existence gained a new perspective in the light of timeless presence, but it wasn't my time to be here.

I felt myself pull back from the brightly lit stage, moving perpendicular to lateral planks of white light beneath me. As I floated backward, the forms of my father and children gave way to the receding light that had encompassed them.

I re-entered my unconscious body, my heart again compressing and releasing at an effortless fifty-five beats per minute. In a few hours, I would awaken, having been deeply imprinted with my journey to the afterlife.

My gift in death was to live within God's greatest gift in life – the gift of love. It had permeated and embraced me, showing me a dimension not obscured by the limits, influences, or misdirection of our world.

To say I'd visited the most beautiful, pure, and undoubtedly real experience imaginable would be inaccurate. This place transcended anything a mind could imagine.

Looking back, I think of the patience of God's words as He conveyed them. It wasn't like, "Hey, we need to make this quick. They're on shock number six back there and they're probably going to pull those defib pads off your chest." He spoke, restored my life, and repaired a brain that hadn't felt the push of a self-generated heartbeat for twenty minutes.

God's conveyance resides as perfection. My instruction served in both simplicity and complexity.

I knew instinctively that the "kindnesses" God spoke about were not exclusively of being kind. They also referred to acts of kindness, whether simple or complex. I see people in this world to whom I don't hold a candle. The selfless consistency of their actions toward others is absolute.

By passing suddenly, I'd been given a gift of sorts, having transitioned from mortality to eternity. I inhabited light and love without having known of the cause of my passing. Weeks later, I would recall only a quick labored gasp before exiting my body.

I didn't look back with remorse at the body or life I'd left behind but embraced my arrival to the exaltation of where I'd transcended. I had dipped a toe into eternity. The indescribable beauty of my soul's ability to feel love validated the next life, and the finite fears of this life no longer existed. I had acquainted with the unquestionable immortality of spirit.

22

Your Heart Stopped

ICU to the Recovery Room

"Squeeze my fingers."

I complied.

"Now move your toes."

I again complied.

Wasn't the doctor supposed to say, "Simon says?"

I woke up confused and disoriented. Minutes earlier, my eyes had opened and moved to study the room rather than stare blankly, indicative of brain function. My body battled the lingering presence of sedatives and fought their soporific pull.

Family and friends anxiously awaited to hear the news.

"Where am I?"

Desiree rounded the ICU hospital bed as my eyes struggled to gain focus.

"What happened?"

"Your heart stopped. We almost lost you."

The words echoed as if spoken from a distance.

The blurry hospital room hung like a shroud and occluded the opulence of the previous stage. I ached to describe where I'd just been.

I'd left one world, rejoined another, and landed hard back into my body. Its demands and discomforts made themselves apparent without hesitation. I became aware of my fragility. As a living and breathing being, I'd been re-inserted into my familiar vessel of flesh and bone. It had proven to be a fragile structure and had a few new complaints.

"I gotta pee. I need to get up."

"You've got a catheter, so just go."

I looked down to take inventory of the array of devices attached to my body.

"My chest feels like it got hit by a truck."

"You had a lot of CPR. You might have some fractured ribs."

A gristly feeling in my sternum confirmed over a thousand chest compressions. The slightest movement of my lungs met with a painful objection. It hurt to breathe.

"Geez, I hate hospitals."

"I knew you'd say that, but I had to call 911. You put up quite a fight. When you finally had a pulse, it took six medics to hold you down."

"Cuz they were taking me to a hospital..." I mumbled.

"You kept trying to pull out the intubation tube."

As I could again breathe on my own, the long tube had since been removed replaced by a throb that encapsulated my throat—rectangular burns left from the defibrillator pads branded my chest and torso.

Thick-headed and groggy, I continued to try to push through the residual haze left by drugs and oxygen deprivation. The clarity of my trip to the hereafter remained etched without the slightest encumbrance. An incontrovertible memory had chiseled into my psyche. I'd been in the presence of God, and He wanted me to remember it.

"It's amazing over there. I saw…"

The meds regained their grip, and I again drifted into sleep. Each time I awoke, I'd ask the same questions and take inventory of the room. I noticed Desiree sway from side to side next to my bed.

"I died," I stated as an observation more than a question.

"Yeah, but you're back."

"The other side, it's wonderful…"

I held the moment as two worlds shared loose borders. A sliver of the previous world still embraced me, but the earthly half of this glass needed a refill. Spiritual bliss had been exchanged for physical pain. Exiting the power of that realm felt uncomfortable and unnatural. The freedom I'd felt outside of my being gave way to soreness within this one, once again encapsulated within a human body named Tom P. Huitema.

"I can see how someone wouldn't want to leave that place. Pure love."

"You'll have to tell me about it."

My condition stabilized as medications flushed from my system. The hospital room flooded with visitors and well-wishers as the news of my sudden cardiac arrest spread.

My memory had endured the battle and remained well intact as mental attachments coupled with the present and past.

Initially, I noticed friends held my eye a moment longer. They searched for a sign of diminishment or listened for a subtle slur. As much as they wanted me to be okay, they couldn't help but casually seek differences from the former me. My wit had remained intact, and my engagement with others attested to an unbroken intellect. Brain damage is common after extended periods of oxygen deprivation and twenty minutes without a pulse dipped deep into that well. My cognitive recovery thus far had been miraculous; it appeared the cheese hadn't slipped off the cracker.

Once this became apparent, the temperament of the hospital room shifted.

At my bedside, an old friend quipped, "Most of us treat our bodies like the floor of a pub, and you, Mr. Fitness, go down like a kamikaze."

From the other side of the room, another buddy chimed in. "Heard they were worried about brain damage. They set the bar pretty low – not like you had much of a brain to lose in the first place."

I showed a slight grimace as a chuckle jabbed at my sternum.

"You still whining about your pigeon chest hurting from CPR?"

"Yours would have crumbled like a cracker," I shot back. "Don't you knuckleheads have jobs? How about one of you go down to the café and grab me a large coffee and an almond croissant?"

A doctor entered the room, not expecting to get caught in the crossfire.

"Hey Tom, tell him everything you know. It won't take long!"

"How about I tell him everything we both know? It won't take any longer."

Badgering and insults flowed like beer through a Shriner. When your friends don't hammer you, it's time to worry.

And at that moment, I knew I was going to be all right.

23

SPIRIT FORM

AFTERLIFE IS KIND OF LIKE A BOX OF CHOCOLATES. YOU NEVER WHAT YOU'RE GONNA GET.

If the afterlife is a symphony, our life in this world hardly qualifies as its prelude. We are, at best, only tuning our instruments here.

"When you died, did you see anything?" is a question I'm often asked.

"Yes, and it's magnificent. Would you like to hear about it?"

Most say yes, some sport a nervous look, and others nod in confident validation. A few say no as if not wanting to peek beneath the wrapping of a future gift.

I initially hesitated when telling others about my afterlife experience. I dodged questions like stepping around puddles after a downpour. I sensed they were searching for validation of their ideology. The last thing I wanted to do was challenge another's lifelong beliefs. What I experienced may contradict beliefs held fast by people of conviction, and I'm hesitant to affect that.

My motive in telling the story is not to steer anyone's ideals. My chronicle does not exist to draw into question another's faith. If it aligns with a doctrine and plants the seeds of positivity, then it's good. If it doesn't, it's still good. My experience is nothing more than my recollection of what happened without the intention of meeting another's interpretation of eternity.

My greatest challenge in describing the afterlife is the limitation of adequate words. It's another dimension, and the utility of my vocabulary is like trying to fill the back of a pickup truck with the entire Sahara Desert. Neither the quantity nor quality of my words can truly portray the absolute essence of the afterlife. I can only describe it within the limits of diction. In this portion of my book, I hope the words are written more through me than of me.

The perspective gained from having died is transformative, and I insisted upon maintaining its greatest purity. When I began putting my thoughts into words, the mailbox filled with several books about those who have had similar encounters. I decided not to read any of them, fearing they would dilute my personal experience. I haven't allowed myself to be influenced by the description written by others who have died and returned.

Outside of that literature, I'd heard stories of near-death experiences of seeing angels, beautiful lights, or hearing exquisite music. I didn't get that deal. I wasn't provided with a VIP angel escort. My spirit knew where to go, and I'm glad I didn't need to ask for directions.

The light I saw didn't appear colorful - just bright, though it had an organized shape and form. It existed to focus my attention away from darkness rather than to illuminate the stage of my experience.

I didn't hear beautiful music, though I've enjoyed hearing it on this Earth. Exquisite compositions already exist. The talent to create that music or pull it from the air is talent already bestowed upon composers and musicians.

I'm not denying what others saw, but I believe that If God created heaven and Earth, He undoubtedly sprinkled some of that beauty here. A brilliant sunset or song is a gift that only requires our attention. The gift exists should we choose to embrace it.

It isn't possible to come back from something like this without being a renewed person. As on Earth, there are things we can't "un-see" or "un-hear"; my flight to the afterlife is something I can't "un-experience," and I've been tattooed by it.

In the afterlife, features existed for me to identify my family. After that, a greater identity was presented by the unique signature of their love.

Its magnitude showered me with peace, wholeness, and tranquility.

The purity of love that I felt was unfiltered and powerful. Love in this world is beautiful, but can be restricted by barriers: fear of loss, fear of no reciprocity, fear of pain, etc. In the afterlife, those barriers don't exist.

Love feels no resistance and embraces us in absolute clarity.

My sampling of the afterlife embodied this immense love in a multitude of flavors. Those flavors exemplify when unimpeded by our human form. When we think about love, it can be applied in many ways. The way we love our children has a different feel than the way we love our companions. Love has a broad definition and an even broader application.

Those flavors are distinct in the afterlife, and our souls' palettes can differentiate. Moreover, they are amplified to the point where we can more accurately identify our love. We can recognize the love others have for each other. The spirit body senses, assigns and identifies the specific character of that love with a unique signature.

I could identify a specific difference between what embraced me while in spirit form. I felt the love of my dad, my children, and their love for each other. I could feel the love of where I was basking. All fell across a spectrum with specific identities. My awakened sense of the afterlife gave me the ability to feel and differentiate them all.

The most magnificent was the love from God. His encompassed not only absolute purity but immeasurable strength and grace. My gift of that journey is a better identity of His love on Earth. It spills over from heaven, accessible and available to all of us in the here and now.

The stage of my afterlife pulls me toward fulfilling my assignments in life. Its power reaches for me when I speak to those who question the hereafter or who've lost loved ones, and I extend its hope, power, and verification of the beauty that exists beyond this realm.

★★★

I was at my father's bedside when he passed, along with my brother and mother. He'd been hit by a car while riding his bike, and his injuries were not mendable. His 83-year-old body had had enough, and his cognitive grasp had begun to fade.

On New Year's Eve of 2010, he lay in hospice, and after nearly a week of little movement, his breath had become choppy. I went to the local supermarket to pick up food for everyone and gathered in the room as we awaited his imminent passing.

During the hours prior, my brother and I recounted the antics of our youth—the room filled with laughter as we made our guilty admissions and told all truths. Happiness and forgiveness filled the room. Having been unresponsive for days, my father occasionally raised his eyebrows. The hospice nurse mentioned that there are often moments of lucidity when a person is near death. Though his face showed little movement, the expression on his brows demonstrated participation in the evening's events.

A few video calls followed from grandchildren and loved ones to say goodbye. The end was unquestionably near. His brows again raised to speak a silent validation.

His breath became increasingly labored during the next hour. As his pulse elevated, the nurse entered the room to check his vital signs. When she positioned herself next to him, my dad expelled a final breath and fell silent. At that moment, I saw what appeared to be a gray mist travel diagonally away from the top of his body.

Stunned, I asked my brother, "Bart, did you see that?"

He'd seen it, too.

My mind quantified possibilities at a scientific level. I didn't bother pursuing an explanation, concluding one had to exist. Given my afterlife experience, today I feel differently about what I saw.

My father and I didn't always see eye to eye. He'd married a stunning woman 13 years his junior who wanted babies and had gotten three of them. My mother's focus had turned toward us, and having minimal skills or interest as a parent, he'd been pushed aside.

His outlet became building and repairing things in the garage, and though he was the last person you'd see at one of our little league baseball games, his expression of regard took a different form.

If I broke something, all I had to do was set it in the garage to find it repaired soon after. His love was expressed through his actions, and though it wasn't a language I understood as a child, it was one in which I would gain fluency later in life.

Though we didn't understand each other back then, we borrowed from one another at a higher level after his passing. I became more mechanically inclined.

In the afterlife, the energy of his youth presented itself. I felt gratitude for his presence and his unity with Hope and Faith. The energy he couldn't direct toward us at an emotional level now resided as an abundant love for them. Coming home to that verified a dimension of heaven.

The burden of our body's necessities frees us in the hereafter; practicing greater attentiveness to the present moment rather than the egoists of material things, desires, regrets, and so on helps create that freedom.

In the living world, we can bog down with everything we wish we had or didn't have. These obstructions don't exist in the afterlife, where time doesn't exist. We are freed from regrets of the past or fears of what is now an infinite future. The events of the afterlife paid no regard to an existence of time. God said what He said with perfect cadence, strength, and calm.

Like a baby born pure without judgment, my rebirth brought me from a pure place to one where I must again re-seek that purity.

It is then that I tap into my additional perspective and renewed faith. It helps me find the path to that better place.

24

EXPLAINING THE UNEXPLAINABLE

BONUS TERRITORY

The ball leaped off the oversized head of my driver. It tracked like an arrow for about a hundred yards followed by a hard right turn, landing well clear of the fairway in an area of high brush.

"I think I saw where it went," I said, hoping I hadn't lost another golf ball.

Jerry grinned as I stowed my club and hopped onto the golf cart.

We returned to the conversation of his unswayable perspective.

"If the afterlife is so wonderful, why don't we all just end our lives here?" he asked.

"Life is a workout, and the hereafter is the warm shower that awaits. You can't cut short the workout. You need to earn the shower."

"What happens to those who do?" he countered.

"We've been given a gift of life, and ending it defeats the purpose of that gift. God didn't ordain me while I was over there," I retorted. "He restarted my heart, reset my brain, and put me back in the game. If I'd been a quicker thinker, I'd probably have asked Him to refresh these knees before He put me back in my body."

"Not the first place you've been kicked out of," he said, laughing. "You should also have asked him for some help with that slice, although I don't know if God could even fix that. So why do you think you have such a vivid recollection?"

"I benefited from a rapid reconnection of brain activity. Lots of folks who have a cardiac arrest lie for weeks or months in a comatose state. Retrieving a memory and reestablishing normal brain function can take years. They may have a similar experience, but their recall may be limited."

"How do you know it wasn't a dream?"

"When you wake up from a dream, you know you've been dreaming. Pieces of the dream usually don't make sense or lack continuity. Your mind wrote a story to which you reacted. It makes sense at the time – at least until you wake up. You're the actor and audience in your own performance. My trip to the first piece of heaven didn't have that. My mind couldn't have randomly created the absolute clarity and magnificence of my journey. My senses activated and amplified. Here in life, we function in an underdeveloped or primitive form at best."

Jerry looked at me with skepticism. He searched for a hole in my experience while I rummaged through the high grass with a seven iron.

"Here's the thing, Jerry," I continued. "You've known me a lot of years, and I've never had a God campaign. I've always hung my faith on a spiritual but not religious hook. Church for weddings and funerals."

"Yeah," he agreed. "I still think it ends here. If it doesn't, we're in bonus territory. You'd actually be in bonus territory if you could hit that ball onto the fairway for once."

My ball had come to rest on a rough patch of land. My swing connected and the Titleist popped toward the green. I sat back on the golf cart and grabbed my water bottle.

"Dude, it's total bonus territory. It took death for me to get a true grasp on life."

"How's that?"

"In that short time, I recognized how we naturally shed the inherent necessities of living inside a physical structure. I had no itches to scratch. In life, natural functions like hunger or thirst exist. Yearnings provoke and direct our thoughts away from internal peace. Whether we're trying to fill the dopamine tank with Facebook likes, getting a sugar fix, or providing ourselves essential service, we're constantly trying to satisfy the wants of our bodies."

I raised my water bottle to exemplify my point.

On that note, we transitioned to a different subject. I had no desire to embark on a recruiting campaign. God has His plan for everyone; my role wasn't atheist conversion. We returned to trading insults like a couple of high school kids. In a friendship injected with quick wit and one-liners, Jerry and I knew how to sharpen our swords. The better the insult, the harder we'd laugh.

We finished the back nine. Another triple digit round. The smell of fresh-cut grass and time with a friend well outweighed my lack of ability.

Walking through the parking lot, I turned on my cell phone and noticed a missed call. Old friends called to check on me, many to hear about my journey. They hadn't called to appease the thoughts of a guy whose beliefs were chiseled by religion but rather to hear the words of someone who once debated its inconsistencies.

"Hey, buddy."

"How are you, Tom?" A slight shake carried in his voice.

"Taking it one beat at a time. You alright?"

Kurt Wein's family tree is rooted deep in aviation history. His grandfather's contribution occupies a corner of the Smithsonian Air and Space Museum. He'd perpetuated the family legacy as an airline pilot who could still name the firing order of an eighty-year-old radial aircraft engine. Kurt had been at the hospital within hours of my cardiac event.

"My dad is going downhill, and he doesn't have long. He won't admit it. Every time the pastor walks into the hospital room, he chases him out, saying he's got the wrong guy."

"I'd expect nothing less."

"I told him your story. It comforted all of us to know where he's going."

"Sometimes I think it's as great a gift to be able to tell people about my experience than to have had it."

Many people had reached out to share stories of family members who struggled with death and dying. I felt honored to help many find some peace.

When cancer patients shed the pain of their bodies or when the elderly climb away from the restrictions of their aged and worn selves, the freedom from those burdens translates to instant bliss. When we suffer, our minds tend to that pain and attempt to resolve it. In the afterlife, we transcend away from the aches, pains, urges, and addictions of the bodies we've worn.

Managing our discomforts on Earth requires a degree of physical and mental discipline. Health, fitness, and a proper diet are a way of easing some of those burdens. We're lighter on our feet, have more abundant energy, and reduce the pull of habits that slow us mentally and physically by lessening the body's distracting demands.

Prayer and meditation create a similar easing of burden, helping us escape the stresses that direct us away from inner peace. It produces an intention and a dialogue that opens a gateway.

In physical death, the greater power of my soul presented itself in its pure and natural form. It's like comparing the sun's light to an incandescent bulb. The attraction I felt to that strength and the love it holds made the desire for earthly possessions feel trivial at best. Its truer wealth reshaped me. From my afterlife perspective, the currency changed.

My experience included God speaking to me and sending me back with a basic instruction. At that point, I departed from a spirit form and returned to my body.

Explanations contrary to a God experience are overwhelmingly thin, and the only true and accurate explanation is to have had an authentic experience with the Almighty. What I experienced couldn't be imagined, devised, or felt by a human body.

That evening, my friend Doc Hansen picked me up in his pontoon boat. The conversation turned toward my cardiac event. He, like some other friends, needed to shape a scientific conclusion.

We cruised the perimeter of Austin Lake, singing along to old rock tunes. The mercy of volume drowned out our poor vocal quality while the therapy of the music remained. When a song played unworthy of increased volume, our conversation re-engaged.

"The brain is a powerful thing, Tom. It was suffocating, and that's its way of responding." With thirty years as an ICU doctor, he'd seen many lives end. Death escorted away the young and old, the rich and poor, and everyone in between. "I'm not saying you didn't see what you saw, but there's got to be an explanation."

True, I thought. *The indiscretion of mortality could hurt*. Doc concluded long ago that his role in saving people required emotional limits. He, like many, assigned logic to my experience. To him, death is the end of life and not a perpetuation.

"Sudden cardiac arrest is sudden death," I countered. "My brain didn't know it was coming. From this, skeptics believe the brain automatically says, 'Quick, play the death reel;' it'll make them feel better. If anything, I'd believe the contrary. The brain doesn't have enough time to react, let alone respond. Consciousness transfers."

"For the sake of argument, let's say there *is* a trigger. Why do those who don't believe in an afterlife have same type of experience? Why would their minds build scenes contrary to or opposite to their lifelong beliefs? Wouldn't they be better served with tropical beaches, a Swiss chalet, or a ride in a Bugatti as their death reel scene? At least a response mechanism that aligns with their engrained mental pathology while fulfilling a lifelong dream or desire, not the opposite."

"My afterlife would be the front row watching Elvis perform," he pondered.

"Let's poke the bear scientifically," I continued. "A vivid experience emanating from a dysfunctional, suffocating, and dying brain doesn't add up. Signatures of gamma activation have been found in comatose patients following cardiac arrest. Studies within the medical community have labeled this as a paradox. That's a nice way of saying that not only can't science explain it, but it runs contrary to a logical outcome. It also points to the possibility of a covert or hidden consciousness at the time of death."

"I haven't seen those studies, but there's got to be an explanation." Doc's logic locked to his methods of conclusion. This world had walls; even scientifically inexplicable phenomena couldn't scale them. To him, the lack of a scientific explanation didn't invite a Godly one. The burden of science needed to exist even if it couldn't.

"In my case, how would my brain know to preprogram a scene denoting people I love, followed by an exit back into my body when I wasn't even aware I'd passed? Again, if a person is aware of their impending passing, some case could be made for this. I lay down, and my heart had stopped unbeknownst to me. I went from 6'5" and bulletproof to dead. Contrarians then believe the mind has a unique protocol to run an afterlife reel if it senses my heart has stopped. And it knew to run the one where I come back into my body after twenty minutes without a pulse and seven blasts from a defibrillator. You think my brain organized the most beautiful and connective scene beyond my imagination and inserts *that*? What I experienced couldn't be assembled by my brain."

"Some neurologists call it one of the biggest mysteries in neuroscience," Doc admitted.

"Strictly by the numbers, my chance of regaining a heartbeat was one in fifty. The chance of returning without brain damage held even more abysmal odds. Yet my brain knew to run the script that brought me back to my body without cognitive impairment."

"I've entertained all the angles I can come up with on this, Doc. A scientific approach doesn't add up to the flawlessness of my experience. It doesn't add up to the clarity of senses, the disposal of what doesn't serve, the magnification of what does, and the perfection of where I went. I believe the brain is powerful, but it couldn't have put that together in a million years, let alone composed it arbitrarily during a sudden death event. I experienced perfection. Perfection can only come from one place, and it's not of this Earth."

Doc nodded with a distant look of contemplation. Like Jerry, he looked for a gap in my story but came up empty.

"Before my temporary death, I see myself as having been both on the right and wrong track. I believed our soul passes beyond this realm but questioned post-life structure. I paid homage to someone or something greater than myself but lacked a real definition."

"Doc, God exists. I didn't return to hand the world an unquestionable and undeniable proof of God, heaven, or even the hereafter. We come here with nothing and leave with nothing. Dipping my toe into the afterlife didn't mean I'd come back with souvenirs. My gift was a glimpse of what awaits. The clarity of my experience and the depth of beautiful love that embraced me is not one I could have experienced in human form. No number of words can even begin to describe its true beauty and clarity."

"Great song. Turn it up!" one of us called and we returned to happily singing along with an 80s melody. Doc played air guitar, challenging my boundaries of non-judgement.

Not every conversation ended with someone gaining a new perspective or hope for the afterlife. Whether heaven or Helsinki, I welcomed their take-it-or-leave-it attitude. Every friend remained a friend. They embraced my return to health and return to the here and now. I felt gratitude that they'd been there for me because their friendship held the wealth that mattered.

25

Reload

Boatbuilding 101

Short final approach.

As we glided over the runway threshold, an automated flight deck voice announced the final 50 feet of my career, counting in increments of 10.

"50, 40, 30…"

I took a deep breath and aimed my visual point of reference at a spot beyond the runway's distant end to aid my depth perception. Left eye dominant, my head turned slightly right as if sighting down a rifle barrel. The balance between thrust reduction and pitch up of the nose had to be perfect to arrest the descent rate at the nanosecond before touchdown. Too much pull and the aircraft could float; too little and the gear would plant firmly. Be the ball; this machine is an extension of me.

A breath of wind quartered from the left of port as we settled our last few feet; I nudged the slightest additional back pressure on the control yoke and closed the thrust levers to idle. The challenge still took concentration after 45 years of practice, and today, it yielded its reward.

The Dreamliner's tires buttered onto the runway as puffs of white smoke appeared and vanished behind the main landing gear. Only the feel of the wheels rotating beneath the passengers announced a connection to the ground.

The aircraft sat pitched upward for a moment longer, poised in a poetic stance before the nose graciously bowed to meet the centerline. Massive lift dumping panels forced themselves upward from the wing, pushing and holding the plane firmly against the pavement. The blow of thrust reversers shook against the firmness of the massive fuselage and tail.

A smooth deceleration brought the airplane to the pace of a brisk walk as it exited the runway. Once clear of the runway, formations of spoilers and flaps neatly retracted like a peacock drawing in its feathers.

We taxied to the ramp where awaiting fire trucks flanked our wingtips. They delivered an aquatic blast from their water cannons, welcoming my final arrival—cake at the gate, tearful goodbyes from co-workers, friends gathering, and an epic retirement party that evening.

Or not.

I'd pre-programmed my departure from the airline industry at age 65 and envisioned it right down my final flight, only for that door to slam shut.

Clayton Moore, who played the Lone Ranger, basked in the remnants of his former glory and held on tight. He often noted that he'd "fallen in love with the Lone Ranger character." It had embraced him like a blanket, and its warmth became inescapable. Moore longed to be revered and recognized. He fought legal battles to retain the right to wear the mask while further attaching himself to the creed of the character.

But it was not the creed of a fictitious character that made him who he was. His persona was real. It's not the mask; it's the person behind it. By comparison, I realized that what I was to others had nothing to do with my uniform. I decided that my reach to them only needed a different avenue, and my passion for inspiring would anchor that creed.

I resolved not to fade away or hang on to the last pieces of my abruptly ended career. The retirement flight could be a couple of garden hoses squirting over a Piper J-3 Cub, followed by beer and cupcakes at the hangar.

Change requires a degree of honesty and personal dialogue. Rather than asking myself what I didn't want, I needed to ask what I did.

In the words of Lao Tzu, "New beginnings are often disguised as painful endings." Faith in a new beginning moves us forward, extending a trembling hand to hold an unknown while releasing a firm and steady grip on what doesn't serve. When someone leaves a relationship, some compare the most special parts of that bond to their expectations of the next while dismissing the reasons for its demise. It can rob the uniqueness of the subsequent experience of its potential glory.

The title of airline captain had seen a premature demise, and trying to reinsert anything into that space would be putting a square peg into a round hole.

As a teenager, I worked as a stock boy at a grocery store. On Saturday evenings, a group of older men would gather outside the store and wait for the early edition of the Sunday paper to arrive. Every week, they stood waiting, rain or shine. Little conversation occurred between them beyond minimal niceties, almost an admission of their common lack of enthusiasm. Soon, a Pittsburgh Press truck would roll up, dropping a stack of thick folded paper slabs stuffed with circulars onto the curb. The guys would each grab a copy of fresh ink and disperse, only to reappear seven days later. I wondered how they balanced and filled the other parts of their lives.

It's necessary to do more than find ways to keep ourselves busy. Something needs to fill the cup.

In my days as a young first officer, more than one soon-to-be retiring captain would drop a piece of advice into my lap. One told me that if he'd worked as hard on his first marriage as he did his third, he'd likely still be with his first wife. He'd also be spending retirement with her and dipping into a bigger bank account.

Another captain shared, "It's like this kid. Ask a captain what he's going to do after he retires, and you'll know how long he's going to live."

"How's that?" I asked.

"Well, it's like this," he continued with marked animation. "If the guy tells you he's going to play some golf and spend time with his grandkids, he's dead. Two years tops. If he tells you he's going to build a boat and sail it around the world, that guy is going to live forever."

He took a bite of an apple and looked out the flight deck window, nodding in agreement with himself. I stored the tidbit in my long-term memory and called upon it today.

The question remained: how can I be the guy who builds the boat, especially after being given a second chance at life?

Life threw me a curveball, but it's a hittable pitch, and that's where the skill lies.

The flight deck of an airliner had been my home for 38 years. I'd planned any subsequent step to involve flying, but with an ICD pacemaker, I couldn't fly a banner tower down the beach.

Some retired pilots don their uniforms and head to the airport. They walk through the terminals assisting passengers. Though I commend their commitment to others, I needed a different form of engagement: less Lone Ranger, more boat builder.

I walked an emotional tightrope and recognized a pang of pending depression. Friends' supportive voices and loving regards had begun to quiet as the shock of my event slowly faded into the past. After the flowers had withered and the only evidence of comfort food showed on my belly, I faced a new reality.

Soon after my cardiac arrest and revival, I felt the bite of the Michigan cold. It made me reclusive. I retreated toward the warmth of seclusion. We live in a time that fortifies and even promotes that seclusion. Rather than associating with humanity, we can click items into a shopping basket, and they'll magically appear at our doorstep soon after.

Life inevitably returns to normal, albeit a new normal. Having worked in the pilot assistance realm with those who struggle, I knew restoring positivity would require daily attention.

The support of my beloved Des was pinnacle, though I knew I could only use that crutch for a short time. During duress, we ask that person to extend their bandwidth to help us, but the time comes when we must relearn to walk.

The most successful relationships are those with two strong and independent individuals. When someone seeks another to fill in the pieces missing within themselves, they stop working on themselves and burden their partner by passing that workload.

I'd been given the gift of life and assigned a task by the Almighty. I made it my goal to find my new path.

26

IN A HEARTBEAT

WINGS AND THINGS

In a heartbeat, life, and life as I knew it, had ended.

Defying the odds, I'd recaptured my earthly existence. An unplanned chapter had inserted itself into the book. In my arrogance and self-assuredness, I'd written the pages ahead, only to see them shredded.

A few weeks after my release from the hospital, I visited with the fire/safety workers who had saved my life.

"I've been doing this for over thirty years," said Clay. "You're the only person I've ever seen that deep into cardiac arrest who came back unscathed."

I thought back to the yoga practice I'd done next to Clay two days before my heart stopped.

"That made twice in the same week that I did a corpse pose next to you. Only the second time I needed a defibrillator."

"You were pretty feisty when you came back, too. You kept swinging at everyone around you like you were in a prize fight."

"Yeah, I had a colorful youth. I may have been resorting to primacy."

I reiterated my gratitude to each of the fire/safety workers. They'd handed me back my life. It was time to take that gift and consider which direction my new path would lead.

When we lose something dear, there's an essential period of mourning and transition.

I wrestled with a complexity that my heart struggled to quantify. I loved my job and flying the Dreamliner, but I needed to contemplate an egoic attachment to the admiration of my position. It had an addictive appeal. The uniform, the aircraft, the authority, and how "I'm headed to Madrid" rolled off the tongue. Combined with social media fame, I pondered the structure I'd stood upon.

I reminded myself not to mourn my ego. It didn't serve me nor did it rightfully occupy a place in this equation. After removing that element, the remaining sentiment was my adoration of flight and how it had fit by way of occupation. It presented the most genuine piece of this experience and what had been yanked out from under me, revealing a former role with which I needed to make peace and bid farewell.

I'd spent about 40 years being "Tom, the Pilot." I can't say I minded it, but I know Tom, the loyal husband, the committed dad, the faithful friend, and the devoted family man, always placed well ahead of that; they are not only labels of more significant substance and importance but also a better answer to whom I strive to be.

My job couldn't love me back. Flying couldn't even love me back. But my friends and family can. Some of my soul-searching meant shining a beam at what qualified and was worthy of higher regard, even if it didn't yield reciprocity. I considered what held me so intimately to all that flies.

I once owned a Piper Super Cub. After each flight, I'd wipe the bugs from the front of the wing. It didn't feel like a chore to clean. If anything, it had a ceremonial appeal. I bonded with my airplane by cupping my hand and running it along the curved and slightly dented shape. I'd connect to the leading edge by envisioning the conception of lift. As the airfoil moves forward, it is from here that tiny air particles are separated and utilized to produce aerial sustenance.

The wing is a selfless workhorse designed to support and serve the fuselage. I regard it not only for its production of lift but for its service to the entire structure. It holds the airframe aloft and asks nothing in return. Whether the dented leading edge of a 50's era utility taildragger or the flex of a massive composite Boeing Dreamliner wing, it's the harmonious concert of airflow to create lift that I hold near and dear.

The love of this creation doesn't require reciprocity – it's art. The Sistine Chapel or the Mona Lisa, don't care what I think of them. I enjoy their beauty and appreciate the hands that created them.

I still gaze at the sky. I'll see a hawk maintain effortless flight on a column of rising air. Feathers shift to shape and embrace the updraft, holding the bird aloft. It attaches to something timeless and authentic. Wings have existed organically for thousands of years and have been harnessed by humanity over the past century.

I didn't need to be Captain Tom to embrace the beauty of flight. I only needed to look up.

27

THE AIRWAY AHEAD

A LEGACY

A group of pilots stand in front of me shoulder-to-shoulder in two rows of five. Each looks toward me with an expression frozen in time. I know their faces well and regard them with deep respect.

"Good morning, gentlemen. I'm going to make you proud today."

I address the entirety of the group and humbly repeat the words I've told them many times before.

"Thank you for all you've done and for entrusting me with your legacy."

I salute them and take a moment to regard the pilots individually, giving each a nod. Two pilots in the back row share an uncanny resemblance, likely brothers or twins. They sport pencil-thin mustaches, their hats tilt sideways in opposite directions, and each cracks a mischievous grin. These are the guys who made everyone laugh. A gentleman returns my stare in the front row with a fatherlike charm. This is the boss, the approachable leader, and the man these other pilots consult for solace. In the front row also stands a kind-faced young man; the third finger of his hand bares a wedding ring. His wife's worries as she and their children wished him a safe trip undoubtedly played into her sleepless nights until he walked back through the door of their home.

As the men stand on the ramp at Chicago's Municipal Airport, one of ten American Airways Curtis Condor II sleeper planes fills the backdrop. The aircraft incorporated many of the latest comfort amenities, including sound insulation and deep cushion seats. It lacked features like anti-icing, weather radar, and pressurization. Between the metal wire-braced fabric bi-wings sit two oil-belching Wright Cyclone engines. Once airborne, the 720 horsepower radial engines pushed the structure through the sky at a cruising speed of nearly 170 mph, touted to be the fastest speed humans had ever traveled.

These aviators traversed unforgiving skies while navigating scarcely traveled airways during commercial aviation's infancy. Five of the ten Condors purchased from the Curtiss Aeroplane and Motor Company crashed, resulting in hull loss. The pilots' skills were to thank for minimal loss of life in a time when airplanes flew on a wing and a prayer. Passengers entrusted their safety to these gentlemen; they stood tall and delivered.

Though the last of these pilots likely died decades ago, I renew my commitment to what they started. My heart and loyalty go to these brave men who handed me my aviation legacy and the responsibility of its perpetuation.

The tarmac upon which they stood is today known as Midway Airport. On the other side of town sat a military base called Orchard Field (ORD), known today as Chicago O'Hare Airport.

The near-life-sized photo in front of me was taken in 1935. It now adorns the wall of the CR Smith Museum in Ft. Worth, Texas. Little did these aviators know they were the forefathers of what would become the largest airline on earth.

Beneath a high airfoil-shaped ceiling, only a few feet away, sits a shiny metallic Douglas DC-3, the Flagship Knoxville. It displays the American Airways livery of the same era. Twelve tables with chairs surround the aircraft, used for interviewing pilot candidates. I've conducted hundreds of interviews in this room.

I've been entrusted with passing the torch these pilots handed me. Their legacy prevails today as my airline nears its one-hundredth birthday. I salute them again, filled with the intention of the task I've been assigned.

28

Four Letter Words

The Art of Interviewing

"Your Chicago-bound flight has encountered unplanned headwinds. Despite a favorable forecast when you departed Rome, Italy, the destination weather continues to deteriorate due to a cold front stalled over the Great Lakes. Dispatch anticipated no delays when they filed the flight plan."

The pilot applicant looked thoughtfully from across the table, absorbing my words.

"Aircraft approaching Chicago O'Hare are stacking up and starting to hold. What are your greatest concerns?" I continued.

He covered a few points, hoping he'd elaborated sufficiently, and glanced across the table expecting validation. We sat quietly, allowing a thick silence to hang between us. I waited. He flashed red, knowing he'd missed a key factor. His answer so far had been canned, smelling of prep services and pilot forums.

"What else?" I pressed.

He returned a blank stare and then searched my eyes with a desperation that said, "I've got nothing." I held a stoic expression and then relented.

"Four letter word." I hinted. "Begins with F. F U E…"

"Fuel!" blurted out the applicant.

"Bingo," I said.

"When Air Traffic Control assigns us the holding pattern, I need to determine my bingo fuel," he said confidently.

My interview partner, Kiersten, raised an eyebrow and glanced at me, imperceptibly shaking her head with an expression of, "You really spoon-fed him that one."

Kiersten probed in a new direction as the applicant continued to struggle. Sweat beaded across his forehead in the cool room. The interview progressed, but he continued to miss essential elements when answering technical questions.

Nice guy, I thought, *but he's nowhere near ready to work for our airline*. Without a word passing between us, Kiersten and I knew our assessment scores would be similar, drawing the same conclusion.

We kept the interview as light-hearted and enjoyable as possible. The letter of rejection he'd soon receive would sting, so we wanted him to look back, knowing he'd been treated with professionalism and respect. Additionally, we'd like him to re-apply once his experience level reached our expectations.

Every month or two the interview team ventures abroad to professional pilot conferences. It's fertile ground for acquiring new talent, so employers from flight schools to the big three airlines attend. Familiar faces fill the halls, and we often greet each other, even comparing notes. The discount carriers are a friendly bunch despite knowing we actively hire away their pilots.

"I'm not sure if I should feel bad about taking away so many of your pilots," I said to Scotty, a recruiter for a discount carrier team.

"I wouldn't worry about it," he said giving me a wink. "If they wanted us to stay, our senior management would give us a better contract. I probably won't be here much longer either."

I'd spent much of the morning doing "meet and greets" at our booth. Pilots came for a quick one on one visit with a member of our team. The equivalent of speed dating, we'd share career advice and take note of stronger applicants we could potentially interview. During my lunch break, I walked around the conference floor, making a swag run. It amounted to filling a bag with pens, hats, key chains, candy, or whatever else vendors gave away. On one occasion, while fishing through a bowl of candy trying to locate a Snicker's mini, a young man approached me.

"You interviewed me and turned me down," he said.

I had a vague recollection of the guy. I'd asked him some questions involving a winter operation scenario and concluded the only ice he'd ever seen was in a margarita.

"Do you have any idea why?" I replied calmly. I'd learned to stand my ground regarding hiring decisions. The airline had fortified its position, even in the face of a pilot shortage. The boss, Captain Cory Glenn, briefed the interview team countless times, reiterating our unwavering hiring standards. "I'll take the heat," he'd say. "Even if that means canceling flights."

"I suppose I could have prepared better," the young man admitted.

"If this is your dream job, continue to gain experience and take it seriously," I encouraged. "When you apply the next time, you may see a different result."

He'd acted graciously after his initial words, understanding that I was his proponent. I wished him success and returned to my hunt through the candy bowl.

No one gets a free pass through the interview process. Sons and daughters of veteran pilots and legacy employees have been turned away. A close friend of the department head was rejected after a weak interview. Pilot interviewers play no favorites, and an over-confident, under-prepared "I got this no matter what" attitude has resulted in countless rejections.

As interviewers, we ask ourselves several questions. Would we put our family on the candidate's airplane? In a world of rapid advancement due to pilot attrition, could they command an airliner after only a short tenure? If the answer to both isn't a resounding "Yes," we can't hire the pilot.

Back at headquarters, in a small office space, Steve Campbell and I sat around a table stacked with piles of logbooks, scouring page after page of the applicant flight histories. They commenced their interviews a short distance away in the CR Smith Museum area. Steve balanced his life as a pilot for AA, an Air Force base commander, and a loyal family man. His disposition always reflected a calm and even temperament.

"Hey Tom, we've got another one," he said from the other side of the pile of logbooks.

Many of our reviews reveal training and checkride failures not disclosed on the application.

"How many?"

"Just one. An initial commercial flight check. He listed an Instrument ride failure but missed this one."

"We'll let him come clean," I said.

We ask pilot candidates to bring their original logbooks dating back to the first time they flew. We review the books and look for training events, endorsements, aircraft flown, and more. It gives us an idea of the pilot's history. We also look for training failure trends.

Almost everybody has had to deal with a bad day. They prepared for a check ride, hoping to complete the qualifications for a new license or rating, only to fail the event. Still, some have had more than others, and it can reveal a less qualified pilot.

One of the most common things we see are pilots who don't disclose failed training events on their application, only to be confronted about them after their interviews. At that point, a simple admission followed by an update to the application could put things back on track, depending upon the nature of the undisclosed details.

Steve and I walked down the hallway to speak with the applicant. He'd completed a successful interview; another minute of our time may have completed the process.

"Mr. Walter, we reviewed your application and compared it to your logbooks. We noticed you had not listed a failed commercial pilot check ride event."

"I didn't list it because that was a written exam," he retorted.

"It says here it was a practical exam."

He became unnerved, quick to respond with a dismissive edge.

"Oh yeah, that was the oral exam before the check flight." His words were quick and clipped.

"This appears to be the flight portion of the exam by looking at the entry in the logbook."

"Oh, that was a discontinuation of the exam because we couldn't finish it and were going to do that part later," he again lied.

Steve maintained his cadence, metering the conversation methodically.

"According to your logbook, you had three additional training days before retaking the flight evaluation, and it appears to be a complete check ride. The failed event is also documented as such. Different documentation would exist for a discontinuation."

At that point, the applicant fell silent. He looked down with sheepish admission, not expecting the level of challenge. The trust of the unknowing is a liar's most useful tool. We'd come armed with the truth, only seeking admission.

"Please update your application to reflect this, Mr. Walter," Steve concluded.

The failure of the ride itself was inconsequential—the list of untruths created the consequence. Walter's interview had gone well, and the balance of his logbooks indicated a well-qualified candidate. He would have received a conditional job offer that day, followed by a background check and a few screening items.

The candidate had worked hard for many years only to lose his dream in the final minute of his interview screening. Not only was the fruition of his dream within reach, but speaking a simple truth or admitting a minor omission could have carried him over the finish line and into a multi-million-dollar career.

We discussed it with the boss behind closed doors. His candid approach reinforced our position.

"If he lies to us here, what will he tell the passengers? How would he handle the logistics of a mechanical discrepancy?"

"We thought the same."

The boss gave us a knowing look.

"You guys already know the answer," he closed.

So close, but yet so far.

Disheartened by the interaction, I returned to the briefing room to continue reviewing logbooks. The table was stacked high with logs belonging to the next group of pilot candidates. We returned to the task at hand, with sets of books of nearly fifty applicants to review in a single day.

★★★

We loaded into a van from the DFW Airport Marriott South to the AA Flight Academy early the following day. Interviewers are mainly pilots based abroad coming in on their days off. We share the hotel and transportation as fellow interviewers and pilot candidates climb aboard. Little did the candidates know that their interview started long before they arrived. Those who demonstrated ill tempers with employees on their inbound flights or yelled at a waitress the night before may have already sealed their fate. Character is who they are when they don't know anyone is watching. Gate agents observing the designation of an applicant's travel code have called the recruitment office to report misconduct.

Some candidates engage in conversation in the van while others quietly center themselves. We respond with cordiality and kindness, hoping to ease their anxiety, having remembered the day we were in the same position. A young man beside me fidgeted nervously, unsure whether to address me. A thin line of dust striped the shoulders of his dark suit. His suit had been hanging for a while. He hasn't been to a wedding, funeral, or interview lately, I thought. I broke the ice, hoping to settle him.

"Where are you coming in from?" I asked.

A short conversation ensued as he recounted his home and the airplane he flies. I wished him the best with his day. I hoped he'd do well and that the next time he pulled his suit from its hangar, it would be for the new hire dinner at our airline. We advocate for our potential pilots, knowing the job is only theirs to lose. They've attained our qualification requirements, and if they've prepared, the interview should be no more than a technicality.

In the briefing room, I studied the application loaded onto the iPad. An Army veteran, a helicopter pilot, served his country and then came back to start logging fixed-wing time. I cannot be biased, but this application had a glimmer. My interview partner and I discussed the applicant and agreed on a direction of fair assessment. The interview started soon after, and our conversation took the path of overcoming challenges.

"We were in a hot zone. I needed to get some wounded soldiers out despite enemy fire. The guys were trapped and wouldn't have made it otherwise," he said.

The heroics of his actions left me speechless and grateful. The balance of the interview revealed a man of absolute decency and integrity. His technical knowledge well exceeded our standards.

My interview partner and I were back in the briefing room soon after. Murmurs of post-interview chatter filled the space as other interviewers completed their assessments. "I can't wait to see him get a job offer," I said.

The day yielded some strong candidates, and we had one more interview to complete.

We begin each interview by telling a little about ourselves to lighten the mood. My words are brief, knowing this is the candidate's time, not mine. The young man sitting across the table from us exuded an aura of kindness and wisdom beyond his years.

"Tell us about yourself," I said.

"My family is from a small village in Sudan," said Thamer. "As a child, I marveled at airplanes and dreamt of being a pilot. I entered an immigration lottery and was awarded citizenship via that lottery. When I came here, I only had the shirt on my back. I drove cabs and swept floors, working every job I could find to pay for my education and flight training."

I looked back at his application to see a long list of menial labor jobs before gaining employment as a charter pilot. His education listed a master's degree. As much as I respected and appreciated his story, I still served as the gatekeeper to the position he sought. He needed to earn this final step.

I've given interviews and scratched my head, wondering how seriously the applicant had made this day. I've also given interviews that left me straining to maintain my composure, filled with the inspiration of the person across from me as they shared their stories of challenge and triumph. Thamer's interview was among the latter.

He crushed it. In every scenario, his answers and elaborations reflected strong knowledge and capability. We awarded him a conditional job offer at American Airlines. Tears filled our eyes as he held the letter inviting him to join our team.

'Where are you headed now?" I asked him.

"To see my mother. She's in hospice, dying of cancer. I want to show her this letter and tell her I've fulfilled my dream." Less than two weeks later, Thamer texted. His mother had passed away, so proud to know her son had achieved his lifelong dream of becoming an American Airlines pilot.

It is people like this to whom I wish to pass the torch. Grateful, hardworking, and humble. They are the capable shoulders upon which I happily place the future of my company and the safety of our passengers.

On the days I feel broken by the malfunctions of my heart, I know I've done something outside of my flying abilities to better the longevity of my trade.

I walk to the back of the museum to the 1935 photo of the pilots and salute them.

"I think I've made you proud today," I say. "Thank you for trusting me with our legacy."

29

THE INFLUENCER

THE RESPONSIBILITY OF RECOGNITION

I looked up from my plate of fried rice to see a young man extending his hand.

"I wanted to say hello and tell you I really enjoy your content."

"Thank you. I hadn't expected the account to grow so quickly. It started as a health and fitness page to pass along tips to fellow crew members, but it took a different direction," I conceded.

"What made you change your mind?"

"Fitness is a passion. But one day, I was at work, and I thought it would be fun to tell everyone about the things I love about my job, the airplane, and flying in general."

"I appreciate that," he said. "My pilot friends at the regional airline follow you, and it keeps us motivated."

"Pilots are kindred spirits. There aren't many people my age posting. I wanted to connect to younger generations and hopefully inspire others."

We parted with another handshake, and I contemplated the implications of recognition within my field. My last few Instagram videos had each neared or exceeded a million views, pushing me to just inside of eighty thousand followers. It filled me with a nervous angst.

The word "followers" left me uneasy. I wanted to connect with others who shared my passion for airplanes. That put them beside me, not following.

As an emerging account, I made mistakes addressing those looking to bolster negativity. No matter how positive the message, someone will have something cutting or negative to say.

I discussed it with my friend, Fernando Contreras, an airline pilot whose social media reached many. His account, fitaviatorsclub, encompassed the health and fitness tips mine lacked.

"I once posted a picture doing a leg raise in the aisle between two passenger seats. It got a ton of hits, but the claws came out. Lots of nasty comments," he said.

"I know we tell each other to ignore that, but it still grinds at you. I think the concept of polite society often ceases to exist in social media. Even the kindest and most inspirational posts get hit by haters who hide behind anonymity. I grew up differently."

My thoughts regressed to my elementary school days.

Despite being the shortest kid in the 6th grade, Timmy O'Donnell could pummel anyone in his class. He happily proved it if you crossed him, combining a thick-limbed fire hydrant physique with a badger's temperament.

The only kid who could possibly take his title was his best friend, giving that battle a low probability of seeing fruition. Since I was a grade junior, I was afforded the chance to respect Timmy from a distance. No one thought of him as a bully, and he dealt his wrath fairly. He was known to slap the bad manners out of kids who hadn't been directed properly at home.

Growing up in the South Hills of Pittsburgh in the 1970s, I learned to choose my words carefully at an early age. When I used the wrong words or if their limited inventory depleted, fists started flying. Sometimes, a wordless act itself invited a scuffle. If someone cut in front of you in the lunch line, for example, they'd better also be able to block your punches. Five minutes later, everybody was buddy-buddy again. I'm not advocating this approach to growing up, but it worked for me and taught me boundaries.

Like many of my generation, social media violated the tenets of my upbringing. I'd spent my life looking people in the eye when I addressed them, and that residue remains etched into my character. The anonymity of words and the cowardly concealment of those who make anonymous cruel comments didn't appeal at all to me. In the words of Mike Tyson, "Social media made y'all way to(sic) comfortable with disrespecting people and not getting punched in the face for it."

Some did get "punched in the face," but in a different context.

At every airline, pulling out a cell phone at the wrong time to take a quick video has cost many pilots their licenses and even their careers.

"Sterile cockpit" refers to a period when no extraneous acts or conversations may occur. It's about the business of the airplane, and that's it.

On a beautiful evening approaching Los Angeles International Airport, the setting sun painted the sky in layers of orange and yellow.

"Oh my, what a sunset," commented the captain. The first officer silently shot the captain a glance. The lack of response was a reminder of the sterile period.

The aircraft descended through 7000 feet, its autopilot still engaged, locked onto horizontal and vertical approach profile. The airliner would soon land on Runway 24L at LAX.

The captain grabbed his cell phone to shoot a quick video. He panned from inside the flight deck and out of the forward windows, capturing the shafts of slanting light pushing between brilliant colors meeting the coastline ahead. He put away the device, and the aircraft continued toward the runway.

"Got it. Wow, what an awesome shot," he said, again violating sterile cockpit.

Excited by the stunning scene he'd videoed, he posted the clip that night to his small social media account. Within days, it met the eyes of thousands, including those of the FAA. The FAA started license action against the captain. He'd captured his own knowing and willing violation of flight regulations, complete with altitude and aircraft registration. It led to a substantial consequence.

With that in mind, I filmed my video clips long before I needed to tend to my job duties. I'd either compose a clip from outside the aircraft or get to the captain's seat well before my assigned sign-in, sitting by myself on the empty flight deck.

I didn't post very often, but when I did, I committed to making every post informative and positive. The page insisted upon positivity, inspiration, and gratitude. I'd laid the welcome mat to those who wished to participate and played an active role to address anyone who posted negativity on my account. Negativity resulted in being restricted or blocked.

Even then, I walked a fine line regarding my airline's social media policy. I feared that going outside those boundaries, even with the best intentions, could result in negative consequences. Social media is the elephant in the room for public brands like airlines. I chose to make friends with the elephant and promised to tread carefully. My airline embraced its positivity, but it took a careful approach to the content parameters.

I related a final post to my position with the pilot interview team, encouraging aspiring pilots to maintain accurate logbooks. The airline insisted upon complete flight histories, and I'd seen numerous applicants run into issues due to poor documentation. It's not as appealing as the inside of a 787 but important to budding young aviators. The responses once again varied.

Some logbook services hopped on board by reposting the video, using the words to reinforce the importance of a tight set of books. Pilot applicants made comments of appreciation.

"Thanks, Captain Tom. This motivated me to go through my logs and make sure everything is correct. I've also passed this along to my pilot friends who will soon be interviewing."

Of course, negativity also made its way to the comment section.

"Hey, Captain, Tom. Looks like pushing paper has made you soft," one comment accused.

"I'm passing along the info so pilots won't see their application process delayed," I answered.

"I flew into ice runways in the Arctic Circle and didn't log it."

"Well, maybe you can go back up there and build an igloo to live in instead of trolling my page," – ENTER. I watched the comment float in front of me for a minute or two. That felt good.

- DELETE

"I respect your experience. I'm sure you bring a lot to the table in your present position." - ENTER

"This isn't me. I'm not this nice," whispered the voice of my inner child. The kid who threw hands in the elementary school lunch line had spoken up.

Despite the positive connection to fellow aviators who strived to someday sit in the left seat of a Dreamliner, a familiar ball sat at the pit of my stomach each time I started to compose a post. The uneasy footing of a slippery slope filled every post; the time had come to back away from social media interactions. Other than promoting airline conferences that I attended, I retreated to the introversion and privacy I'd once had.

A year later, the account still idles, hovering near 75,000 followers, awaiting its next post.

30

GREAT CIRCLE ROUTE

ENDING IN THE BEGINNING

High above the jagged terrain of a sparsely populated area we guided our single engine Cessna through a series of training maneuvers.

"My controls," I said as my right palm cupped the flight control yoke.

I asked the student to lower his head and close his eyes as I pulled the airplane in several directions to throw off his equilibrium.

"Your controls."

He looked up to see the ground spinning toward him.

"Whoa!"

"As you can tell, we're in a spiraling dive. Get us out of it," I said calmly.

The airplane whined as it raced downward, but we'd started the maneuver at a safe altitude, allowing him plenty of room to regain control plus a sizable margin of error.

"Damn, this is nuts," said the student as he began pulling back on the controls.

"Reduce the power first," I coaxed. "If you pull back, it'll only tighten the spiral."

He throttled back, and the airspeed stabilized.

"Now neutralize the bank angle. I know it all feels odd, and there's a lot going on."

He leveled the wings with the nose still pointed in a steep pitch toward the ground well below.

"How's that?" he asked, adding back pressure to the flight controls.

"Easy, you don't want to overstress the airframe."

The student eased the airplane out of the dive as the Cessna 182 returned to level flight. The rapid rise and fall of his breath hinted stress though a look of resolve signaled new learning.

"Let's duck into Temecula and grab something to eat. You look like you need a break," I offered.

We entered left traffic to the French Valley Airport, landed south, parked, and walked across the ramp to the airport restaurant. The student, Spencer, is one of my closest friends, and his child, Sydney Skye, is my Goddaughter. He had gotten enough of a workout, and we'd checked all the required squares. The price of the beating was lunch.

We ordered, then debriefed the details of our flight lesson. Something about flying increases my appetite, though I wouldn't be choking down a salty crew meal today.

"That's a pretty tricky maneuver," Spencer said. "Good thing you don't have to do that kind of stuff in a 787."

"Actually, we do. Upset recovery is a part of every training cycle. Not only that, but they'll distract us in the simulator and then flip the airplane over. Whether it's a Cessna or a Boeing, you need to know how to recover."

We continued talking about the nuances of nose-high and nose-low recoveries as the waitress slid a club sandwich and fries under my nose.

"We're going to go do it again," I said. "But this time we'll be recovering by referencing the flight instruments."

My friends knew a flight review with me would be intensive. If anything, I'd work them harder because their families, the families I love, could be on their airplanes. I wanted to make sure they knew what they were doing and couldn't forgive myself if they didn't. My long and winding aviation path had lost many friends along the way.

Forty years and millions of flight miles after leaving the Allegheny County Airport as a flight instructor, the great circle of life brought me back to where it had all started. I'd renewed my Certified Flight Instructor certificate two years earlier at Brown's Seaplane Base in Winter Haven, Florida. The reward came along with a seaplane rating, which amounted to splashing around the inland lakes of Central Florida for several days, followed by two thorough and complete check rides.

Flight instruction beckoned, and even without a medical certificate, I could teach advanced levels of aviation to licensed pilots. The joy of flying small airplanes reeled me in, greeting me with the familiarity of primacy. I thought about the first lesson I'd taken at fourteen, needing to sit on pillows because I couldn't see over the dash. I'd learned to fly an airplane before I knew how to drive a car. The aircraft had become a tighter squeeze after a growth spurt a short time later. My now sixty-year-old body had lengthened and broadened, but the fit of the airplane was otherwise the same. The welcome feel of a small aircraft touched a deep part of me.

Pilots long for the sky and are mesmerized by flight modalities, eagerly distracted by everything from hummingbirds to helicopters. We're happy to admit to being geeks and embrace the humorous banter associated with our passion. We answer the call of the sky and with all who share it. Whether a budding student learning the basics or a forty-year aviation veteran, the commonality of our love to touch the heavens unites us in spirit.

Months later, on a hazy summer afternoon, Spencer departed the Catalina Airport and turned his Cessna toward the California coastline. Wildfires had obscured visibility and blended the ocean and sky, no longer revealing a distinct horizon line. Without an adequate visual reference, the aircraft continued to roll into a dangerous bank angle and dropped into a nose low attitude. Remembering what he'd learned, Spencer scanned his instruments and correctly assessed the condition. He rolled the wings level and returned the airplane to a correct pitch. The training may very well have saved his life.

31

WHAT CHANGED AND WHAT DIDN'T

FILLING THE DASH.

My close friends and I share a saying. "If you're not *living*, you're not living."

We spout it out randomly, but usually amid hysterics. It calls us out on the present moment and reminds us to live and love life. High fives, knuckle bumps, and raised glasses share the moment.

The shock of my temporary end would have been worse had I looked back at an unfulfilled existence. Losing your life isn't as bad as never having lived it.

The dash between the dates of birth and death is the only place where life and its magic can happen.

Banksy is quoted as saying, "They say you die twice. One time when you stop breathing and a second time, a bit later on when somebody says your name for the last time".

I'd contend that the digital age immortalizes us. On a distant day, a family archivist will retrieve their genealogy and might find a pic of a person holding a fish caught while standing along a swift and hurried river. They might find a person perched at the top of a mountain, breathing in the view. They might also find that person slumped and soaked in boisterous inebriation.

A future historian could discover a picture of them standing tall as a part of an organization they once belonged to. In that moment, centuries from now, someone would resuscitate their name, giving it another breath of life. By Banksy's definition, I'd contend our second death will only be at the collective passing of our digital humanity.

What would we like our uber-grandchildren to see centuries from now? A life lived, a life inspired, or a life wasted?

I've made it my task to make the images viewed twenty-five generations from now one that shows a life lived and inspired, not for them but for myself. Confronting death shouldn't be the reason or motivation for living life, though it strengthened my resolve to hit some items on the bucket list before I kick the bucket. Again.

It's often assumed a brush with death stokes appreciation for life. Those who have gone through near-death experiences are peppered with perspective. Not everyone who visits the afterlife writes a motivational memoir, but those who've seen what awaits are given a gift. It's a glimpse of eternity, and those who embrace it often use it to contribute to humanity.

With that in mind, I wrestled with a few life choices after my event and considered how I have and haven't lived my best life. Coming face to face with mortality can be sobering. I've seen long lists of regrets made by those on their deathbeds. Some did all the right things, but still had life taken away from them at far too early an age.

I wondered how I flatlined before Keith Richards of The Rolling Stones. He was born with a filterless cigarette in his mouth nearly twenty years before me. For decades, he drank like a fish and injected himself with every form of poison imaginable. All the while, he deprived his body of essential nutrients. Richards put himself on death's door more times than he could count, only to watch his less rebellious fellow band member Charlie Watts be the first to pass. Richards contended, "The body serves," having been gifted with physical resilience. Most of us don't get that same gift of resilience.

When passing fast-food restaurants, I notice long lines of cars at the double drive-through lining up for high-fat, low-nutrition forms of sustenance. I considered that I could have smoked, drank, and eaten the worst foods and possibly lived beyond 60. Had my discipline been in vain?

I'd had abundant energy because of a healthier lifestyle. When others began to tire, I continued to maintain stamina. Rather than watch my children from the sidelines, I coached and practiced alongside them. I'll always prefer a surfboard on a wave over a chair on the beach. Movement has given me happiness. By not living a sedentary life, I have been given the privilege of diverse experiences, whether hiking up a hill or paddling on the water. Beyond the fitness aspect, I'd been rewarded with a connection to like-minded acquaintances.

My gym buddy, Steve Hutson, came by to spend the afternoon, go for a boat ride, and talk about life. His contagious laugh had quieted though he'd still stop mid-workout to regard anyone who offered their greeting, never inconvenienced.

After taking the pontoon boat for a lap around Austin Lake, we walked up the stairs to the house. He'd expelled every ounce of energy, coughing and wheezing. I would have offered to help had I known his condition had declined this much.

"Sit and catch your breath; we don't need to be anywhere but right here," I said, still surprised by his weakened state. He'd been at the gym only a few days earlier.

We took in the view while a cool lake breeze pushed away the afternoon heat.

"The cancer is spreading to other areas of my body," he said.

"I pray that you'll beat it."

"I'm at peace with dying." A calm acceptance presented in his expression, his voice steady and without fear as he spoke through labored vocal cords. I could tell he meant it.

"It's beautiful there," I said, holding but not pushing my glimpse. A shimmer in my heart told me he'd see that eternity.

The cancer continued its aggressive attack, metastasizing throughout Steve's body.

"Love ya, buddy," he soon wrote in a text after being moved to hospice.

"Love you, too, brother."

Did my peek behind the curtain of eternity lessen my distress when Steve died? Not entirely. It provided a blanket on a night that I needed two. I knew I'd miss him, his laugh, and his friendship.

Coming back from heaven gave me perspective but didn't provide me immunity from pain. On days when life and love are hard, I pull from the strength of faith to rebuild upon shaken foundations.

I'm often asked what I learned and what I've changed. What I learned is that God is real. An inventory of what we do on Earth deposits itself in the afterlife. Having been given a second chance at life, I press myself to a higher standard. I made the team once, but I can't hang my hat on that. I'd hate to mess that up now that I've been put back in the game. Writing this book has reinforced my connection to the hereafter. God hasn't given me an "attaboy," but on the days I'm shaken by the thought of my cardiac arrest, the power of where I went re-installs inner peace.

Many people in this world find God through faith. They find Him through His creation. That's all the proof they need. They get it. In tapping that, they have found their peace.

I speak to God daily and notice a slight change in perspective. My prayers are of gratitude and are often followed by asking for courage and strength. I keep it foundational and try not to allow my prayers to resemble Santa's wish list. God's challenge is His plan, which is the plan for my courage and strength. I've been given ways to earn it.

My time here is once again just that: time. And that provides me with a task while I'm here on Earth – to continue filling the dash.

32

EAR OPENER

GOING WITH THE FLOW

"Listen to the silence. It has so much to say." -Rumi
"Try listening to some music. It makes time go faster." -Amazon Alexa

A thick white contrail painted a line across the sky high above. "I wonder where they're headed?"
"Who knows?" answered Des." Our cell phones are back in the car where they belong. You can put your head back up in the clouds later. For now, enjoy this beautiful day."
We'd rented kayaks to enjoy an outing at Kings Landing in Central Florida. Soon after paddling away from the hustle and bustle of the tourist-filled landing area, we found ourselves floating through a place of peace and solitude. The gentle flow of the river eased us along. We fell silent, embracing the beauty of nature as it gently presented itself. I pulled up my oar and watched it drip. Each droplet met the water and formed a small concentric ripple. Time slowed to a crawl.

A soft whistle of wind spoke through the grasses lining the river's edge. The peace brought us to our breath while heightening our senses.

"Boomba, boomba, boomba." A pair of kayaks approached from behind. The music blaring from a subwoofer was only bullied by loud conversation as they paddled furiously down the river.

I could relate. As a young man my music was the unfiltered sound of jet engines. Their song had left their mark with upper range hearing loss.

In a world inundated with sensory input, many chose to overpower calm rather than invite its rare tranquility. The sound of silence is a melody that requires an adept and accepting ear.

The noisy kayaks passed, their fading sound giving way to the awaiting serenity. A gator laid motionless on a bog enjoying the sun's warmth. Turtles perched side by side on the protruding branch of a fallen tree while tiny silver fish scurried in the clear water beneath them.

Our oars again raised from the river, pausing propulsion to extend the moments of peace.

In one direction, the river pushed us along. In the other, it challenged us to paddle against its movement. Headwinds are a bonus when you're not eager to land. I concluded the faster I flew, the sooner the ride ended, and often throttled back a small airplane not to save gas but to extend my time aloft. It's not the notes but the space between them that creates the cadence of a beautiful song.

33

THE TRIPLE CROWN

THE RIGHT SIDE OF BED

The American Airlines Skyview 6 coffee shop opens for business at 6 a.m. The building, an in-house 600-room employee hotel, nestles within the American Airlines corporate campus. I'd crawled out of bed five minutes earlier, put on a pair of sweats, and navigated my way downstairs to the counter of the coffee shop. When I approached, I noticed a gentleman standing back, looking up at the menu. I jokingly stepped in front of him.

"You weren't in line, were you?" I said, looking back with a smile, then stepped to the side.

The man insisted I go ahead of him as he hadn't yet made his choice of beverage. We exchanged niceties as I offered to buy his coffee.

"Thanks so much," Allan said with an embracing smile.

"The gift is mine."

A spirited and inspirational conversation followed. Allan had survived a heart attack a few years earlier, having also beaten significant odds. His energy and positivity illuminated the rest of the morning, reminding me that even the most subtle choices can make or break the direction of our day.

I'd made my bed, extended a small act of kindness, and made a friend, giving me another reason to thank God for the gift of this day—a Triple Crown before I'd even wiped the sleep from my eyes.

On my three-minute walk back to my room, I passed by another person who'd been given a unique direction from God. Reverend Derrick offered his morning greeting, nearing the end of his all-night shift. He towered at 6'2", 270 lbs., wearing a red security guard shirt and khakis. Despite his proportions, his welcoming presence never falters. He meets every person's eye with invitation and compassion.

"Good morning, Reverend. How's everything?"

"Blessed and highly favored." It's how he always answers.

"Tell me something you're grateful for."

He fires off six items faster than the speed of thought. We share pleasantries and the warmth of a common perspective. After being nearly killed in a car accident and lying in a coma for eleven days, he rejoined the world to put his hands on others with God's intention. Though his path differs from mine, he has been assigned a task and fulfills it daily.

Finding our path doesn't require a trip to the gates of heaven. The truly gifted are those whose faith already puts them on that path.

I once admired an old diesel motorhome at a gas station and complimented the owner, giving kudos for keeping a rig of this vintage roadworthy.

"I growed up workin' on 'em," he said with an endearing disposition. "Vacation should start when ya leave the driveway, not when ya git to the campground."

I couldn't agree more with this gentleman's wisdom. In the spirit of life being a journey and not a destination, I remind myself not to wait to enjoy myself, let alone be happy. Happiness is readily available through pure and simple interactions with others.

That evening, back at the Skyview, I'm enjoying dinner at the Landings cafeteria with Captain Jim Glick and Area Director of Flight Captain Tim Raynor. Tim had called nearly every day after my cardiac arrest and inspired much of what I've written. We're joined by a few Chicago-based pilots I've known for many years. My friend Alex sits in front of a pile of food. He's lean and fit, yet he puts away the groceries like no one I've ever seen. We can't help but rib him a little.

"Alex, are you going to eat all that?"

"Heck, yeah. This is just a Scooby snack for me."

I look at the others. "He's like one of those boa constrictors that eats a deer. At first, you're like – there's no way that'll fit. Then he unlocks his jaw, and the next thing you know, it's a big lump in his stomach. The only difference is the snake can hardly move while Alex will go run a 5K."

Alex takes the badgering well, and we share a laugh among old friends.

The conversation turns to what I didn't do before my brush with death that I plan to do now.

"What lessons did you learn?"

A remnant of my pilot assistance experience reveals itself.

"Your heart shouldn't have to stop for you to find your own definition of happiness. I was already content."

"The old adage is that if you fall off a horse you just get back on. But if it's an overly spirited horse and keeps throwing you off, you may not have been meant to ride that one. There's no shame in going back to the barn to find a different horse that could put you on a different path."

"It's not realistic to drop everything and go scale Mt. Everest if climbing never interested you. Why build a boat to sail around the world if you get seasick? I try not to fill my cup with someone else's favorite flavor."

"Then what do you plan to do?"

"I'm going to hit those white sandy beaches, tour the castles and enjoy the views. But the highlight reel will end, and I'll eventually come home. I'll keep a social structure - run around with Des, spend time with my children, or hang out with friends. Beyond that, I'll build and create. From nail guns to novels, I won't sit idle. When I've looked forward to the 'good part,' I didn't always realize I'd already arrived. This moment is a 'good part'. I'm sitting here laughing with old friends."

The words affirmed views they already held.

I consider my daily foundations may seem inconsequential or inconvenient, but their rewards have paid exponentially.

I try to stir three elements into my day that I refer to as my Triple Crown. Borrowing from the insight of Admiral William McRaven, I make my bed the moment I get up as the act invokes a task-oriented mindset for the day. My second element is to express gratitude. It's a list of anything I can think of, from the bed I just got out of to the roof over my head. When I draw attention to what I might deem inconsequential it creates a mindset that causes me to notice what I'd otherwise overlook. It rewires me to see and appreciate little things and reinforces a more positive perspective of life when I notice them repeatedly. The third is to do something for someone, whether big or small. Add an arrow to someone's quiver to edify their faith in humanity.

Even if it's a bad day, that night, I get into a made bed, grateful for a day of life, knowing I tried to make the world a better place. The Triple Crown routine is sometimes only a single or double crown, but the wins have outnumbered the losses, and that steers my life toward contentment.

34

SOMEDAY

THE BEGINNING AT THE END

"I hope that someday you have a job and are not in jail."

My mom had set a low expectation for me. I attributed my abysmal 1.7 GPA to razor-sharp vision. In most of my high school classes, that vision meant choosing to sit next to a diligent smart kid. During exams, I'd glance at their answers to pass tests for which I hadn't studied.

I admired the school bus driver because he could leave after dropping us off. My mind found tranquility when it drifted outside the walls of my school. On a warm spring day, I tuned out the class lecture, staring hypnotically out the window. I watched a gull spiraling upon a current of air, barely flapping its wings. *Birds had it good*, I thought. *Free to fly and not locked down inside a dusty building for hours a day.*

"Tom!" The teacher's voice cut through my daydream.

"Yes?" I answered, redirecting my attention to the chalkboard.

"You're never going to get anywhere looking out a window," she said.

Maybe, maybe not, I thought.

My classmate, Andrew Bernstein, turned to me and asked, "Why do you seem to enjoy not learning?" I couldn't answer him then, but the question stuck with me. Andrew topped the class and would become a successful lawyer and even a winning contestant on *Jeopardy*. As much as his question carried a stab, its intent hit deeper. Copying his test answers may have helped me pass a class but the lazy act left me on the losing end of the bargain. I'd learned nothing.

It wasn't that I didn't have a desire to learn. I simply needed to have a choice in what I learned.

I'd recognized my love for flying early in life, asking to be taken to the airport to watch airplanes as my birthday present. I recently saw a movie clip of our family dating to the late 1960s. While my brother and I chased each other around the observation deck, an American Airlines Boeing 727-100 entered the frame making its way across the tarmac to an awaiting gate. Little did I know I'd command the flight deck of that airplane nearly a quarter century later.

Airplanes saved me. They refocused a blurry and rebellious childhood. They gave my brain a reason to learn and an elation in that learning. The aviation community embraced me.

Today, I look back at a life filled with purpose and look forward to its continuation with appreciation for each beat of a heart that once stopped. Recent surgery to repair my heart issues gives me some reassurance of a normal lifespan. The gifts and challenges of this life or the beauty of what awaits beyond this life center me between heaven and Earth. Wherever I end up, I know this: it's a good place. I wish you all the beauty of both.

Epilogue

I check the EKG function of my smart watch several times each day. Not long ago, the readings jumped erratically, mirroring a distressed heart function. I willed the device to show thirty seconds without a hiccup, but that didn't happen. An ICD / Pacemaker mounted beneath the skin above my left pectoral muscle stood by, ready to deliver a lifesaving shock.

There were nights when tears would come instead of sleep. I had forgotten the blessing of each living moment, instead replacing those moments with unfounded sadness. I'd scold myself for feeling anguish that had no right to exist. My prayers would reconnect me to my faith, like eyes adjusting to a darkened room.

"We'll never know what happened to you, and there's a good chance it could happen again," was not an acceptable diagnosis. I needed to know why my heart stopped.

Five cardiologists later, the correct prognosis awaited inside the doors of the Mayo Clinic, thanks to a superior medical staff armed with state-of-the-art diagnostic devices.

I'd found the right path but still met obstacles. One of those took the form of an aging and testy cardiologist whose pointed words took an accusatory shape.

"Do you have *anything* else you want to tell me?" asked the doctor. He searched my face with suspicion.

"Yeah, don't buy Bitcoin." That's what I *wanted* to say, but a filter turned it into, "I hope to fly again." I regretted exposing my fragile motives the moment the words left my lips. He leaped at the opportunity to turn the knife.

"You can't drive a school bus or even a truck, let alone sit at the controls of an airliner," he said. I met his eye, feeling the venom in his words but not giving him the benefit of a reaction. He looked for emotion and found none. The insensitivity of his statement strengthened my resolve.

Survival was about persistence and perseverance, and it led me to answers.

Soon after, I met a cheerful advocate whose disposition should serve as the framework for other physicians.

We spent part of the consultation telling "dad humor" airline jokes.

"What does DELTA stand for?"

"Don't Expect Luggage To Arrive!"

"How about, Doesn't Ever Leave The Airport!"

Few things are funnier to me than two baby boomers belly-laughing at each other's corny jokes.

Dr. R. Scott Wright assessed my condition and made a viable diagnosis. A significant heart valve issue had allowed blood to reverse flow, causing dangerous expansion of the chambers.

"You appear to be a perfect candidate for a robotic surgery to repair your mitral valves," he said.

That's what happened next. Collapse the right lung, stop the heart, fix the issue, restart the heart, reinflate the lung, and call it a day.

The valve surgery proved very successful, and my EKG now told a different story. Peaks and valleys ticked and spaced perfectly. A metronome of cardiac muscles did their job, no longer pushing severe regurgitation into the left atrium. The issue had been addressed, but had my heart healed?

Three months later, I sat at the cafeteria of the Mayo Clinic, awaiting the results of an echocardiogram from two hours earlier. A nervous chill lined my stomach, awaiting the moment of truth.

'NEW TEST RESULT' popped up on my cell phone.

Tears filled my eyes as I read the diagnosis. All heart chambers had rewarded the repair by remodeling to near normal size. My heart now pumped a percussion of near-perfect cadence and flow.

I walked outside and looked into the brisk Minnesota sky with renewed hope. Would I again build my nest in the captain's seat of a Boeing Dreamliner? The child inside awaited the moment he could again stare back at a beautifully flexed wingtip. Maybe I could tow a banner down the beach. I'd be happy about anything that put me back into the air. The young fellow within needed a plane ride.

I retreated to Costa Rica, scouted a nice surfing spot, and paddled out to catch some waves. I delayed my entry into the choppy Pacific water, taking notice of a rogue set that had just swept over a small group of surfers. Some caught the waves, and others were run through the spin cycle beneath their crushing force. Referred to by surfers as "getting caught on the inside," their longboards had too much buoyancy to duck under the breaks, leaving the surfers at the mercy of the tumbling water. *Hold your breath and take the beating*, I thought. *That first gasp of air can be thirty seconds away, but it's priceless.* One by one, their heads popped out of the foamy backwash, swimming toward their boards before the next wave bore down upon them.

I navigated between the sets and, once beyond the wave line, sat up on my surfboard to catch my breath. I enjoyed a ceremonial moment of gratitude, considering all the places I find God's work. In life and in death, His strength and power are everywhere.

Like other friends who'd survived cardiac arrest, it was the proximity of good fortune and the grace of God that saved us. We'd been given a reprieve beyond that final breath, allowed to come back up for air.

No matter what the future holds, I'll be grateful to have been given a second chance to live and breathe, but I will always long to say six words.

"Hello, this is your captain speaking."

Printed in Great Britain
by Amazon